Ancient Rome

An Enthralling Overview of Roman History, Starting From the Romulus and Remus Myth through the Republic to the Fall of the Roman Empire

© Copyright 2021

All Rights Reserved. No part of this book may be reproduced in any form without permission in writing from the author. Reviewers may quote brief passages in reviews.

Disclaimer: No part of this publication may be reproduced or transmitted in any form or by any means, mechanical or electronic, including photocopying or recording, or by any information storage and retrieval system, or transmitted by email without permission in writing from the publisher.

While all attempts have been made to verify the information provided in this publication, neither the author nor the publisher assumes any responsibility for errors, omissions or contrary interpretations of the subject matter herein.

This book is for entertainment purposes only. The views expressed are those of the author alone, and should not be taken as expert instruction or commands. The reader is responsible for his or her own actions.

Adherence to all applicable laws and regulations, including international, federal, state and local laws governing professional licensing, business practices, advertising and all other aspects of doing business in the US, Canada, UK or any other jurisdiction is the sole responsibility of the purchaser or reader.

Neither the author nor the publisher assumes any responsibility or liability whatsoever on the behalf of the purchaser or reader of these materials. Any perceived slight of any individual or organization is purely unintentional.

Free limited time bonus

Stop for a moment. We have a free bonus set up for you. The problem is this: we forget 90% of everything that we read after 7 days. Crazy fact, right? Here's the solution: we've created a printable, 1-page pdf summary for this book that you're reading now. All you have to do to get your free pdf summary is to go to the following website: **https://livetolearn.lpages.co/enthrallinghistory/**

Once you do, it will be intuitive. Enjoy, and thank you!

Contents

INTRODUCTION 1
PART ONE: ROMAN FOUNDATIONS AND MONARCHY
(753 TO 509 BC) 9
    CHAPTER 1: THE FIRST ROMAN MYTHS 10
    CHAPTER 2: ALBA LONGA, ROME'S ANCESTRAL CITY 25
    CHAPTER 3: FROM THE FOUNDING OF ROME TO THE
    LAST KING 35
PART TWO: THE ROMAN REPUBLIC (509 TO 27 BC) 49
    CHAPTER 4: THE REPUBLIC'S ESTABLISHMENT 50
    CHAPTER 5: THE WARS OF CENTRAL ITALY 64
    CHAPTER 6: EXPANSION TO THE SOUTH 78
    CHAPTER 7: THE PUNIC WARS 91
    CHAPTER 8: ROME VERSUS GREECE 104
    CHAPTER 9: THE CIVIL WARS 118
PART THREE: THE PRINCIPATE (27 BC – AD 235) 138
    CHAPTER 10: THE JULIO – CLAUDIAN DYNASTY 139
    CHAPTER 11: THE FLAVIANS AND THE ANTONINES 156
    CHAPTER 12: THE SEVERAN DYNASTY 171
PART FOUR: FINAL YEARS, SEPARATION, AND FALL
(AD 235-476) 186
    CHAPTER 13: AN EMPIRE IN CRISIS 187

CHAPTER 14: DIOCLETIAN AND CONSTANTINE THE
GREAT 200
CHAPTER 15: THE CONSTANTINIAN DYNASTY AND THE
FALL OF THE WEST 213
CONCLUSION 226
HERE'S ANOTHER BOOK BY ENTHRALLING HISTORY
THAT YOU MIGHT LIKE 234
FREE LIMITED TIME BONUS 235

Introduction

He was supposed to kill the babies. That had been the king's order – *throw the babies in.* Instead, the guard left them in the basket and nudged it into the swollen river.

"Let the gods decide," he breathed, watching the churning Tiber carry the basket out of sight.

Miraculously, the twins survived their voyage down the raging river, and one established the great city of Rome, with an astonishing history that now spans 28 centuries. Called the *Eternal City* by the poet Tibullus, Rome grew into a massive empire stretching from Britain to the Middle East and south to Africa. Rome's culture and institutions profoundly influenced the territories it ruled, leaving an enduring legacy of religion, language, governmental structure, law, philosophy, architecture, and art that continues to impact civilizations around the world.

In this history of Rome, we will unwrap the intriguing myths of the twins and their ancestors and then explore Rome's earliest recorded accounts. Was the founder a feral wolf-child? Who was the mastermind of Rome's unique senatorial system, and how did it function? What propelled the city's rise to supremacy over parts of three continents? Were some emperors genuinely psychotic? Did

Nero murder two of his wives and marry a boy? What was the *Pax Romana,* and why was it so important? Which factors influenced the Roman Empire's ultimate fall?

The second temple of Hera, also called the Poseidon temple, in Paestum, Campania, Italy, provides an example of Doric columns. Norbert Nagel / Wikimedia Commons, License: CC BY-SA 3.0.
https://commons.wikimedia.org/wiki/File:Hera_temple_II_-_Paestum_-_Poseidonia_-_July_13th_2013_-_08.jpg

This extensive and comprehensive examination of Ancient Rome will reveal how all the drama, politics, and empire-building unfolded. It will describe the distinguishing pillars of this awe-inspiring empire, what made it extraordinary, and how the Roman culture continues to influence today's society. Readers will acquire an in-depth understanding of how Rome influenced judiciary systems and left its mark on the culture and languages of Europe. We will explore how the Latin language, the empire's vast and excellent road system, and the *Pax Romana* enhanced the spread of Christianity – even while the emperors were feeding Christians to the lions.

With all the volumes written about Ancient Rome, why write another one? This enthralling overview is remarkably comprehensive, covering the essential information on this compelling civilization. This fascinating and easy-to-understand account will keep the reader turning pages; rather than dry facts, this history provides the captivating stories of the people who built Rome and made it what it was. Some of these individuals were exemplary and ingenious, while others were chaotically destructive. Still, they all played a part in the intrigue and internecine conflict that defined Rome.

Understanding history has multiple benefits. We require an accurate understanding of the past to wisely decide for our present and future. Valuable lessons can be gleaned from the rise and fall of extraordinary civilizations. How have they contributed to who we are today? Some stories inspire and motivate us, and others serve as cautionary tales.

An excellent grasp of Rome's history will help readers understand how today's political systems originated and how the Greco-Roman polytheism developed and influenced Rome until a carpenter and several fishermen transformed the empire and the world. Readers will discover how safe, efficient transportation influences trade, wealth, information, religion, and cultural blending. Through investigating the leaders and emperors of Rome, we can appreciate the heights that good leaders can take a civilization and the depths into which poor leaders can plunge them.

Aneas fleeing Troy, carrying his father on his back, accompanied by his wife and son. Pottery circa 510-500 BC
https://commons.wikimedia.org/wiki/File:Aeneas_fleeing_from_Troy,_olpe,_Greek,_Attic,_525-500_BC,_terracotta,_black_figure_-_Sackler_Museum_-_Harvard_University_-_DSC01697.jpg

Now, let's take sneak peeks into what lies ahead! This overview of Ancient Rome is divided into four sections. Part one explores the mythological foundations of Rome, picking up with Aeneas as he fled the burning Troy, carrying his father on his back. We will follow the Trojan survivors' long trek over land and sea to Italy. How did a Vestal Virgin mysteriously become pregnant, and why were her baby sons, heirs to the throne, fed to the river? We will discover how Rome was established initially as a monarchy, how abuse of power by tyrannical kings led to a democratic republic, and how they finally ended up with an autocracy led by emperors.

When unwrapping these ancient Roman myths, we should remember that myth isn't fantasy. In pre-literate societies or when written accounts are lost through a catastrophe, the oral transmission of ancient incidents may acquire mythological qualities over time. Historical accounts often transform into myths as the stories are retold and embellished. Real people, especially great war heroes and exemplary leaders, become mythologized over the centuries, transitioning into gods or demi-gods.

Dionysius of Halicarnassus wrote "Roman Antiquities," a collection of 20 books that narrated Rome's history from Aeneas to the First Punic War. https://commons.wikimedia.org/wiki/File:Dionigi_di_Alicarnasso.jpg

As we examine the origin myths of Rome – the stories of Aeneas, Remus, and Romulus – our primary ancient sources are *The Aeneid* by Virgil (first century BC), *Roman Antiquities* by Dionysius of Halicarnassus (first century BC), *Moralia: Fortuna Romanorum* by Plutarch (first century AD), and *Roman History* by Cassius Dio (third century AD). Virgil, Dionysius, Plutarch, and Dio all based their works on oral tradition and older manuscripts available in their day.

Our three oldest sources include the *Hymn to Aphrodite* (seventh century BC), an account of Aeneas's conception, Homer's *Iliad* (eighth century BC), which tells of Aeneas's exploits in the Trojan War, and several pieces of ancient artwork and pottery depicting Aeneas carrying his father out of Troy, dating to the sixth century BC.

Part Two, the Roman Republic, focuses on the new Republic's establishment, immense expansion, and internal unrest. We will investigate how Rome conquered nearby city-states and then was invaded and sacked by the Celts. How did Rome rise from the ashes to reassert its dominant power in the region, then face off against war elephants in the Pyrrhic War? We will follow the Roman conquerors through the incredible Punic Wars against ancient Carthage's Phoenicians when Rome gained territory on the Mediterranean coast, the Adriatic Sea, and northern Africa. We will analyze how Rome's successful wars in Greece enabled the empire's ascendency over the Macedonian kingdom and Corinth's Achaean League. Finally, we will delve into the brutal civil wars and social unrest in Rome, the great slave revolt under Spartacus, the First Triumvirate, and Caesar's dictatorship and assassination.

Part Three, the Principate, begins with Octavianus amassing great power and transforming the Republic into a far-reaching empire, leading to his title of *Augustus*. During his reign, a baby was born in the Roman province of Judaea who would transfigure Rome and the world. Augustus was followed by Rome's more notorious emperors, such as the unhinged Caligula, who made his horse a priest, and Caligula's nephew Nero, who lit his garden with Christians turned into human torches. What did Rome do about the Great Jewish Revolt? Which canny strategies led to the conquest of Britain, and how did the five good emperors lift Rome to its peak of power and prosperity? What factors contributed to Rome's decline in the Severan Dynasty.

Part Four surveys ancient Rome's final years – how the Roman Empire split and eventually collapsed. How did wars, internal chaos, barbarian invasions, and peasant rebellions weaken Rome until it was divided into four emperors? We will see how Constantine the Great rose to dominance, becoming sole emperor, breaking the persecution of Christians, and receiving baptism on his deathbed. What contributed to Christianity's expansion throughout the empire? We will discuss why the empire split into eastern and western factions and how the repeated invasions of Visigoths, Vandals, Huns, and Saxons brought Rome to its knees, ending with Romulus' abdication in AD 476.

Now, let's travel back through the distant shadows of time to when a goddess desired a humble shepherd and gave birth to Aeneas, the great champion of Troy whose descendants founded the vast and breathtaking Roman Empire.

PART ONE: ROMAN FOUNDATIONS AND MONARCHY
(753 to 509 BC)

Chapter 1: The First Roman Myths

Aphrodite, the goddess of love and lover of smiles, was mischievously causing the gods to fall in love with mortal women, so Zeus retaliated by filling her with desire for the handsome Anchises, who was herding his cattle on Mount Ida's peak. Burning with lust, Aphrodite wrapped herself in golden finery and came to Anchises as he was playing his lyre.

Overwhelmed by her beauty, Anchises vowed that neither man nor god could keep him from taking her at once. Pretending to be a virgin and a mortal, Aphrodite permitted him to make love to her. From this liaison, Aphrodite conceived, giving birth to Aeneas. When the boy was five, Aphrodite brought him to his father Anchises to raise him in Troy.

The *Iliad* relates how Aeneas fought bravely in the Trojan War as the principal lieutenant to his cousin Hector, the oldest son of King Priam. His goddess mother intently watched over the battle, occasionally intervening to save him from death. Even the gods supporting the Greeks gave him aid, recognizing he would be a king of the Trojans. A king of Trojans but not a king of Troy, as Troy would soon go up in flames.

"Aeneas! Wake up! Wake up now!"

Aeneas awakened to the gruesome ghost of his cousin Prince Hector, covered with blood after his death at the hands of Achilles. "Get up now, Aeneas! The Greeks are storming the city. Escape now – with your family! There's nothing you can do. King Priam and Troy are lost. But you can make a new Troy. You need to leave now! Build a city elsewhere!"

Aeneas initially reached for his weapons and dashed out to defend Troy. He fought with zeal, but witnessing King Priam's death, he realized it was a losing battle. Finally, he hurried home to save his family. Carrying his father Anchises on his back, holding his son Ascanius' hand, and his wife Creusa following behind, Aeneas and his family narrowly escaped the Greek warriors overrunning the streets of Troy. After running out of the city gates, Aeneas looked back and was horrified to see his wife wasn't there. She had fallen behind! He rushed back into the city and met Creusa's ghost – she had been killed by the Greek warriors.

The ghost of Creusa guided Aeneas. Giuseppe Maria Mitelli, from Carracci's frescoed frieze in Palazzo Fava, Bologna.
https://commons.wikimedia.org/wiki/File:Enea_e_l%27ombra_di_Creusa.jpg

"Hurry! Escape to Italy!" Creusa urged him. "You have a long journey ahead, but in Italy, you will be a king and married to royalty."

Weeping, Aeneas stumbled out of the burning city, narrowly eluding the Greeks, to rejoin his father and son and the other survivors who had escaped from the city in time. As dawn arrived, Aeneas led the refugees to the summit of Mount Ida. They looked down to see black smoke rising from their beloved city Troy. Where would they go from here?

The Trojans built a fleet of 20 ships and set sail, crossing the Aegean Sea and landing in Thrace, where they built a settlement named Aeneadae. One day, Aeneas found the body of Prince Polydorus, son of King Priam of Troy. Polydorus's ghost warned Aeneas, "Leave this place! The king of Thrace murdered me! He's shifted his alliances to the Greeks. You're not safe here."

After giving Polydorus proper funeral rites, the Trojans set sail again, reaching the island of Delos, where they discovered a temple to Apollo. Needing direction, Aeneas prayed to Apollo, asking where they should go. Apollo cryptically told him, "Seek the land of your forefathers – of your ancient mother."

Aeneas interpreted this to mean the isle of Crete, the birthplace of Teucer, Troy's first king. Sailing to Crete, they built a city named Pergamum, but then a plague hit the exiles, decimating the Trojans and even killing their crops. Aeneas was confused; he was so sure Crete would be their new home. That night, the *Penates* – the household gods they had brought from Troy – came to Aeneas in a dream, saying, "Crete is the wrong place! This isn't where Apollo meant you to go."

Aeneas discussed his vision with his father Anchises, who reminded him of his wife Creusa's forgotten prophecy: "Go to Italy!"

A Harpy was a predatory monster with a woman's head and body with bird wings and claws. https://commons.wikimedia.org/wiki/File:Harpi.PNG

Aeneas and the Trojans set sail from Crete. A raging storm engulfed them for three cataclysmic days until they found harbor in the Strophades island group. Seeing a herd of cattle, the hungry Trojans slaughtered them to eat, when suddenly Harpies attacked them. The Harpy Celaeno ordered them, "Leave my island! Go look for Italy. When you reach your destination, you will be so famished you will eat your tables!"

Eat their tables? At this odd but alarming omen, the Trojans quickly fled the island and sailed on. Arriving in Buthrotum (in present-day Albania), they joyfully reunited with another son of King Priam, Prince Helenus, who was a prophet. He was ruling with his sister-in-law Andromache, who was still grieving her husband, Prince Hector.

Helenus advised Aeneas of their upcoming challenges: "Be careful to avoid the sea monster Scylla and the Charybdis whirlpool! You should consult the Sibyl [priestess] of Cumae." Helenus then prophesied, "When you find a white sow with 30 piglets, that's the place! Establish your city there. In that place, your descendants will prosper and go on to rule the entire known world."

After exchanging gifts and bidding their old friends farewell, Aeneas and his fellow Trojans sailed to Sicily, where Mount Etna was spewing fire and smoke. A man in tattered clothing ran up to them; he was Achaemenidës, and he came from Odysseus's ship, who had been their enemy in the Trojan War. Achaemenidës had accidentally been left behind when his crewmates were fleeing the one-eyed Cyclops. "Please! I beg you. Kill me now, or take me with you! My life hiding out from these Cyclopes is unbearable!"

Achaemenidës begs for either death or protection from the Cyclopes. Engraving by Giuseppe Zocchi.
https://commons.wikimedia.org/wiki/File:Achaemenides_and_Polyphemus.jpg

Just then, the Cyclopes appeared, and the Trojans rushed to their ships, bringing Achaemenidës with them. Sailing around the coast of Sicily, they came to Drepanum, where Anchises died. After mourning his father, Aeneas sailed toward the mainland of Italy. But once again, they were thrown off course by a fierce storm that drove them away from Italy and south to northern Africa. Finally, they arrived on a peaceful beach. Aeneas scouted the area, hopeful that the 12 ships lost in the storm had found their way to these shores, but he found no trace of them.

The next day, while exploring more of the coast, Aeneas encountered men busily building a new city, reminding him of a hive of bees. Aeneas learned they had recently arrived from Tyre (in Lebanon). They were fleeing their queen's brother, Pygmalion, who had usurped her throne and killed her husband, Sychaeus. Their queen's name was Dido, and they were building the city of Carthage.

Aeneas described the Fall of Troy and their wanderings to Queen Dido. By Jacopo Amigoni.
https://commons.wikimedia.org/wiki/File:Jacopo_Amigoni_(c.1682-1752)_-_Aeneas_and_Achates_Wafted_in_a_Cloud_before_Dido,_Queen_of_Carthage,_with_C upid_at_Her_Feet_-_772276_-_National_Trust.jpg

Wandering through the city, Aeneas entered a newly built temple to Juno and wept when he saw a mural depicting the Trojan War, showing the death of his friend Hector. At that moment, Queen Dido walked in, inviting Aeneas and his companions to join her for a feast that night. Aeneas told her how moved he was by the mural, and the queen recalled the shared history of Troy and Tyre. She told Aeneas he and his refugees were welcome to settle with her people in the new city of Carthage.

Leaving the temple, Aeneas was ecstatic to see his lost ships sailing into the harbor. They had made it! Ilioneus, one of his pilots, reminded Aeneas of their quest to reach Italy, saying he intended to head that way soon. At the feast that night, Aeneas told Dido all about their travels from Troy. Enchanted with Aeneas, the queen repeated her invitation to settle in Carthage. The attractive Dido mesmerized Aeneas, who was rapidly forgetting his mission to build a kingdom in Italy.

One day, they were hunting together when a storm broke, forcing them to quickly take shelter in a nearby cave, where they made love. Dido felt this meant they were married, and Aeneas was happy to stay in Africa with the beautiful queen. The Trojans worked alongside the people of Tyre to build Carthage. Finally, the god Jupiter sent Mercury to remind Aeneas of his foreordained destiny to become a ruler in Italy.

Aeneas couldn't bear the thought of leaving Dido, but he didn't dare disobey the gods. When Dido saw Aeneas's people preparing their ships for departure, she was shattered, vowing suicide if Aeneas left. Aeneas's ships slipped out before dawn, and Queen Dido awakened to discover him gone. She ordered a funeral pyre built, lay down on it, and stabbed herself after prophesying unending strife between Aeneas's people and Carthage.

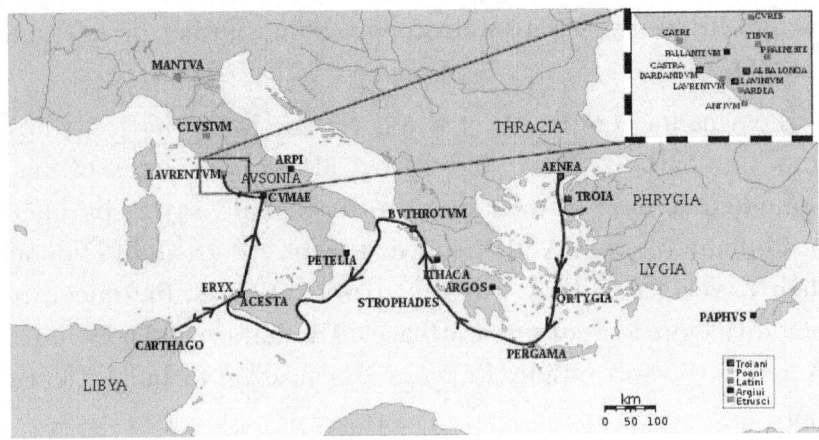

Aeneas fled Troy, first sailing to Thrace, then around the coast of Greece to Sicily, then to Carthage in Africa, back to Sicily, and finally Italy. https://commons.wikimedia.org/wiki/File:Aeneae_exsilia.svg

As the Trojan fleet sailed toward Italy, Aeneas's navigator, Palinurus, pointed to black clouds in the distance. Another storm! They changed course toward Sicily to avoid the storm on the open seas. In honor of the anniversary of his father's death, Aeneas called for a celebration of Anchises's life. But while the men were enjoying themselves with games, the women were plotting trouble.

What were the ladies up to? They were fed up with endless wandering, storms at sea, Harpies, Cyclopes, and volcanoes. They were ready to settle down for good, right where they were. They felt the best way to make that happen was to get rid of the ships, so they set them on fire. Aeneas rushed toward the harbor, praying to Jupiter, and a sudden downpour quenched the fire. Aeneas announced that whoever wanted to settle in Sicily could stay behind. That night, his father's ghost came to him, telling Aeneas to visit him in the underworld before going to Latium.

Finally! After sailing across the Tyrrhenian Sea, the Trojans arrived in Cumae, on Italy's western coast. Aeneas sought the Sibyl (priestess) in the caves, who prophesied, "Aeneas! You and your fellow Trojans will face great adversities in Latium. You will experience another war like the Trojan War."

Aeneas and the Sibyl of Cumae enter the underworld. Drawing by Giovanni Francesco Romanelli.
https://commons.wikimedia.org/wiki/File:Aeneas_and_the_Cumaean_Sibyl_Entering_the_Infernal_Regions_MET_DP811379.jpg

Aeneas pressured the Sibyl to guide him to the underworld. He saw Queen Dido in the land of fallen lovers, but she glared at him coldly. In the land of fallen warriors, he saw both Greek and Trojan warriors from the Trojan War. In the green fields of Elysium, Aeneas was reunited with his father, Anchises. His father showed him a line of souls waiting to return to earth.

"Look, Aeneas! These men will be your descendants! They will be reincarnated as the rulers of your city. There! That's Silvius - he will be your son. And this is Romulus; he will be the founder of Rome. That's Pompey the Great - he will transform your kingdom into an empire. Over there is Augustus Caesar and Julius Caesar - they will be great emperors."

Eventually, the Sibyl led Aeneas back to the land of the living, and the Trojans continued sailing north along Italy's shoreline. Reaching the river Tiber, they sailed upstream. These were King Latinus's lands; he had no sons, but he had one beautiful daughter with many suitors. While performing sacrifices, Latinus received a prophecy: he should marry his daughter, Lavinia, to a foreigner – this man would make the Latin name famous.

Meanwhile, Aeneas's fleet laid anchor off Laurentum, where they set up their tents on the beach and gathered fruit to eat. Before sitting down, they placed wild parsley and dry wheat cakes on the sand to keep the fruit clean. They were ravenous, so after eating the fruit, they nibbled on the parsley and wheat cakes until somebody exclaimed, "Look, everyone! We even ate our table!"

The prophecy of the Harpy Celaeno had been fulfilled! And it wasn't as horrible as they expected. They laughed and shouted with joy – they had reached their destination! Aeneas announced a sacrifice to the gods. Dancing and singing, they brought their idols out of the ship and prepared to sacrifice a pig. The large white sow suddenly broke free, running into the forest. Remembering the prophecy of Helenus, Aeneas followed the pig from a distance until she threw herself down in exhaustion on a hilltop.

When Aeneas (with his son Ascanius) found the white sow with 30 piglets, he knew he had arrived at his destination.
https://commons.wikimedia.org/wiki/File:Aeneas_Latium_BM_GR1927.12-12.1.jpg

Looking around him, Aeneas felt the area was an unlikely spot to build a great city. It was a little too far from the sea and close to an immense swamp. But the next morning, the sow gave birth to 30 piglets, fulfilling Helenus's prophecy. This was the place! This was where the Trojans would build their city.

They set out to explore and came to the city of Latium. Aeneas sent envoys into the city with gifts and assurances to King Latinus that the Trojans came in peace. They told the king about the Trojan War, vowing that if he permitted them to live in his kingdom, they would work for him and help protect the kingdom. Remembering the prophecy about his daughter Lavinia marrying a foreigner, King Latinus welcomed Aeneas and made a treaty: the Trojans could have land for a city, and in return, they would help the Latins fight any enemies.

With the treaty settled, the Trojans built a city on the land where the sow had given birth to 30 piglets. The Latins helped build the town, which Aeneas named Lavinium after Lavinia, who King Latinus had promised to him in marriage. When Queen Amata heard Latinus was planning to marry her daughter to a stranger, she implored her husband not to force this marriage, but Latinus was adamant. Amata flew into a rage. She shared her indignation with the other women, inciting an uproar, then hustled Lavinia off to hide her in the mountains.

Queen Amata was not the only one distraught over Latinus's plans. King Turnus of the Rutuli kingdom had been planning to marry Lavinia. Upon hearing Latinus had promised her to another man, he declared war on the Trojans. Meanwhile, Aeneas's son Ascanius was hunting in the woods and wounded a stag. He didn't realize the deer was a pet of a Latin herdsman. The stag staggered home before dying, enraging the Latins.

The Latin herdsmen attacked Ascanius, and the Trojans rushed to his aid, killing many Latins. The grieving shepherds carried their dead to the palace and laid them at King Latinus's feet, pleading with him to evict the Trojans from their land. Latinus did not want to engage in battle with the Trojans – they'd just made a treaty! But everyone cried out for war, and the loudest proponents were Queen Amata and the women. Unable to calm his people – and sensing the destiny of the gods – the king retreated to his rooms.

Meanwhile, Turnus had amassed a huge army that was marching toward the Trojans, who were in a tight spot. They weren't strong enough to resist the Rutuli on their own, and even though they had made a treaty with the Latins, these people were declaring war against them. Aeneas quickly set about making allies with Turnus's enemies. King Evander (a Greek from Arcadia who had recently settled in Italy) offered aid against their common enemy and sent armies led by his son, Prince Pallas. King Evander also rallied the friendly neighboring kingdoms, and they marched toward Latium.

An epic war ensued between the Trojans and their allies against King Turnus and the Latins. Aeneas and Prince Pallas become close friends in the struggle. Pallas was a great warrior and killed every man he encountered until Turnus impaled Pallas with his spear, ripping off his belt as a trophy. Hearing of the death of his friend Pallas, Aeneas flew into a rage, vowing vengeance. He killed many of their enemies, but Turnus jumped into the river Tiber and escaped.

The Latins suffered a great loss of their people in the war. They built pyres to burn their dead, wailing and lamenting, cursing Turnus and the war. King Latinus reminded his people how misguided it was to fight the Trojans; they should have honored the treaty they had made.

The next day, King Latinus, King Turnus, Aeneas, and his son Ascanius rode out to the battleground. Aeneas swore an oath: if Turnus were victorious, the Trojans would leave Italy. If Aeneas were victorious, the Trojans would live together peacefully with the Latins. King Latinus renewed his treaty with Aeneas. Turnus suggested they end the war with a duel between him and Aeneas to spare the lives of the other warriors.

King Turnus pleads for his life from Aeneus. By Luca Giordano, 17^h century, Palazzo Corsini, Florence.
https://commons.wikimedia.org/wiki/File:Aeneas_and_Turnus.jpg

The two men faced off alone. Turnus grabbed an enormous rock, hurling it at Aeneas, but missed. Aeneas threw his spear, which pierced through Turnus's shield and into his thigh. Turnus fell to the ground, and as Aeneas stood over him, Turnus begged for mercy, telling Aeneas he could have Lavinia. Aeneas paused for a moment, considering, then saw the belt of his friend Pallas on Turnus's waist. Enraged, Aeneas thrust his sword into Turnus's heart, ending the war.

Peace at last! The Trojans and Latins joined as one. Lavinia and Aeneas married, and the Trojans took the language and customs of the Latins. They freely intermarried until the people of Troy no longer called themselves Trojans but Latins.

Two years later, King Latinus died, and Aeneas became king of the Latins. After ruling for three years, Aeneas disappeared during a battle against the Rutuli. No one knew what happened to him, but everyone assumed he must have died. He left behind his wife, Lavinia, pregnant with their first child.

Aeneas was succeeded by his oldest son, Ascanius. Thirty years after arriving in Italy, King Ascanius built a new city, which he called *Alba Longa* (long white town), between a towering mountain and a deep lake offering protection on both sides. In the plains below the city lay fertile land for growing the best wine and fruit in all of Italy.

Chapter 2: Alba Longa, Rome's Ancestral City

Lavinia was in a dilemma. Her husband, King Aeneas, had disappeared while fighting King Mezentius of the Etruscans. Some said he was dead. But where was his body? Others said he had become a god; indeed, he was half-god already. It was all a mystery, but now she was due to give birth any day, with no husband to be found. The city needed a ruler, and her stepson Ascanius, her husband's son from his first wife, had assumed the throne.

What would happen to her now? More importantly, what would happen to her unborn child? Would her stepson give her protection? Or would he fear her power and lineage? How did he feel about this child about to be born? Would he perceive the child as a contender for the throne against his sons? The more she considered the situation, the more alarmed she felt.

She confided her fears to Tyrrhenus, one of her father's most trusted friends and the lead herdsman for the royal swine. The herdsmen had no great love for the Trojans, and especially not for Ascanius – they still carried a grudge that he'd killed their pet stag. As she explained her fears, Tyrrhenus nodded. "My lady, we have no idea what these Trojans will do. The wisest course of action is to go into hiding. I will help you and protect you until it is safe for you and your child."

The next day, Tyrrhenus spirited Lavinia out of the city, dressed in commoner's clothing. No one gave her a second look. He led her into the forest and up into the mountains, where he built a house for her; only a trusted few knew about it. Lavinia gave birth to a boy, and Tyrrhenus named him Silvius – for the forest in which he was born. Tyrrhenus helped rear the boy, and when Silvius was old enough, he joined the king's herdsmen. Few knew his identity. For 38 years, Silvius lived in the forest with his mother.

Meanwhile, his older half-brother Ascanius was facing his own crisis as the new king of Lavinium. King Mezentius of the Etruscans, the Latins' perennial enemy, was pressing his advantage against the inexperienced king and marching toward Lavinium! Within days, Mezentius had surrounded the city with his forces. The people of Lavinium were quickly running out of food and fresh water. In desperate straits, Ascanius had no choice but to surrender to Mezentius, agreeing to pay a yearly tribute.

Many years later, Ascanius broke free from the Etruscan overlords. Ascanius fell upon King Mezentius and his army, taking them unaware. He killed Lausus, son of Mezentius, and vanquished the Etruscan army. Now the tables were turned, and Mezentius had to pay tribute to Ascanius. But that day would be a long time coming.

For now, Ascanius stood on the wall of Lavinium, built by his father on a hill five years earlier. He gazed at the dense laurel forest to the north – the Silva Laurentina – with no inkling his younger brother was hidden away there. Ascanius turned to the south, where the wetlands of the Pontine Marshes lay. He slapped a mosquito and frowned. The *miasmas* (vapors) arising from the stagnant waters caused intermittent fevers among his people, killing one in five. He cursed the *malus aria* (bad air) of the place. He cursed the great white sow who had given birth on this hill, impelling his father to build a city in an unhealthy, unfertile place.

Ex-voto statues in Lavinium. By Contewiki - Own work, CC BY-SA 3.0, https://commons.wikimedia.org/w/index.php?curid=12683615

What would Ascanius have thought if he knew Lavinium would endure with no significant break in habitation right through the next three thousand years? Today, the town is known as *Pratica di Mare* and still has a Roman gate and sits surrounded by the ruins of the ancient city. Over the millennia, attempts were made to drain and fill in the malarial wetland; those endeavors were completed by the engineers of Benito Mussolini in 1939, making the Pontine Marshes the Pontine Fields.

During the 38 years that Ascanius reigned, Lavinium's population continued to grow quickly, but the city lacked arable land to feed a large population. The Latins scorned the mosquito-infested marshlands, so Ascanius established a new capital in a better location. He built the new city on the slope of *Mons Albanus* (Mount Alba), about 12 miles southeast of present-day Rome, and resettled 600 families in 1151 BC. Some say the city's name Alba Longa (*long white*) was after the large, white sow Aeneas had found. Others say it was because of the long, narrow ridge with white walls and houses which ran along between the mountain and the lake.

On the left side of this silver denarius coin struck in Rome in 106 BC are the Penates gods. The reverse depicts the white sow of the prophecy.
https://en.wikipedia.org/wiki/Lavinium#/media/File:AR_serrate_denarius_of_C._Sulpicius_C._f._Galba.jpg

A curious incident happened after Ascanius built Alba Longa. When his family had escaped from Troy, his grandfather Anchises was clinging to the household gods (*Penates*). They were the guardians of Trojan culture and family life and an embodiment of the past. When the ghost of Prince Hector had come to Aeneas to warn him to escape Troy, he'd told him to take his family and the Penates.

These idols had spoken to Aeneas in a dream, redirecting him to Italy. Aeneas had carried them with him throughout his wanderings until he arrived in Lavinium. According to Dionysius, Aeneas built a shrine for them at the highest point of Lavinium's hill, implying that they were no longer just family idols, but gods for the whole Trojan remnant. By bringing them to Italy, they aligned Aeneas's new city with Troy and his ancestors' traditions.

Twenty-five years after Aeneas supposedly died, Ascanius moved the Penates to the newly built city of Alba Longa. One morning, he woke up to find the images gone. Who would have taken them? And then he received the baffling news that the Penates were back in

Lavinium! He brought the household gods back to Alba Longa, and the same thing happened – they returned to Lavinium, apparently by themselves.

After that, the Penates were left in Lavinium, in their shrine built by Aeneas. Although Alba Longa became the political capital, Lavinium continued as a sacred religious center, even after Alba Longa fell to Rome. According to the fourth-century Roman writer, Symmachus, Lavinium continued as a municipal town as late as AD 391, where new Roman praetors and consuls customarily came to offer sacrifices to the Penates and Vesta when they entered their new offices. This indicates the importance of the Penates in linking the Romans to their Trojan ancestors; they were preserved for at least 1500 years.

The worship of Vesta began in Lavinium (brought from Troy) and continued in Alba Longa after it was built. Vesta was the virgin goddess of the hearth and family. She rarely had idols or images depicting her; she was represented by the fire in her temple. The worship of Vesta was one of the longest-lived pagan cults of Rome, enduring into AD 391 when her temple was closed and her sacred flame extinguished by Emperor Theodosius I.

Vesta was considered the purest of the Roman gods, not engaging in quarreling and drama with the others; she had very few myths about her. Her temple could only be entered by the Vestal Virgins, her white-robed priestesses, who remained celibate and kept the eternal flame burning. Besides the shrine for Vesta that Aeneas erected in Lavinium, Ascanius also built a temple to Vesta in Alba Longa.

Ascanius built a shrine to Jupiter on Mount Alban's peak, overlooking Alba Longa. Each year, he invited all the cities that belonged to the Latin League to gather in Alba Longa to worship Jupiter, sacrificing and eating a white bull. Jupiter, the god of the sky and thunder, was king of the gods in Latin, Greek, and Roman mythology. He was often associated with an eagle holding a thunderbolt in its claws. The eagle became an emblem of the Roman military.

All that is left of Alba Longa today are the remnants of the ancient walls. It was built on a ridge running out from Mount Alban's base and extending north. The side of the ridge facing the lake was steep, offering good natural protection. Peperino, a volcanic stone, was the primary building material. One can still see the ancient quarries in the valley between Alba and Marino.

After ruling for 38 years from Lavinium (and later from Alba Longa), Ascanius died. Who would succeed him? Many assumed it would be Iulus, Ascanius's oldest son. But the Latins asked what had happened to Queen Lavinia, daughter of King Latinus and wife of Aeneas. No one had seen her since Ascanius had succeeded his father's throne. And wasn't she pregnant when Aeneas disappeared? Where was that baby? If that child were a boy, wouldn't he have a greater claim to the throne as a son of both the Latin and Trojan royal lines?

Everyone made a big fuss about finding Lavinia. Rumors circulated that Ascanius had murdered his stepmother and her child. Finally, the herder Tyrrhenus came forward and explained what he had done and that Queen Lavinia and her son, Prince Silvius, were unharmed. They had hidden in the forest all these years. He brought them out of the forest and to Alba Longa.

Prince Iulus, the oldest son of King Ascanius, contested Silvius' right to the throne. But the Latins had an election, and Silvius won the vote. He was double-royal, grandson of King Latinus of the Latins and son of King Aeneas of the Trojans. His mother, Lavinia, was heiress to the Latin kingdom, as King Latinus had no sons. Silvius represented both the Latins and Trojans of the kingdom.

After living in the forest for 38 years as a herder, Silvius assumed the throne of Alba Longa, ruling over the Latins and Trojans for 29 years. He appointed his mother as the queen of Lavinium, the city named after Lavinia by her late husband. Silvius named his son Aeneas, after his grandfather, and he ruled the Latins for 31 years.

Ascanius' other son Iulus (or Julus), nephew to Silvius, became a priest. His clan became known as the *Gens Julia* (or Julians), one of the most important patrician families in Ancient Rome, from whom Julius Caesar descended. Dionysius said this family was relocated to Rome after the third Roman king, Tullus Hostilius, destroyed Alba Longa. However, some Julians were living in Rome from its inception, as Senator Proculus Julius announced that Romulus had become the god Quirinus.

Aeneas's descendants, through his youngest son Silvius, ruled Alba Longa for the rest of its history, with Silvius becoming the family surname. One of his descendants, Romulus Silvius (also known as Aremulus or Alladius), was notorious for his tyranny and arrogance. He made himself odious to the gods by forcing the people to worship him as a deity and by using technology to imitate lightning and the sounds of thunderclaps to terrify his people. Finally, the gods had enough of the pretender and sent rain and lightning down on his palace in Alba Longa. The lake rose higher than it ever had, flooding the palace, killing everyone inside, and permanently submerging it. Even today, if the lake is clear and still, the ruins of ancient porticoes appear in the depths.

Tiberinus' grandson, King Proca, had two sons: Numitor and Amulius. And with Numitor's daughter, we move from the history of the Latins in Lavinium and Alba Longa to the birth of Rome. When King Proca died, his oldest son Numitor succeeded the throne, but his younger brother Amulius was plotting to usurp the throne. First, while on a hunting expedition, there was a "tragic accident" in which Numitor's only son Aegestes was killed. With the male heir gone, Amulius organized a coup d'état and stole the throne from his brother. He didn't kill Numitor, just sent him into exile. But Amulius was worried about his brother's daughter, Rhea Silvia.

What if Rhea Silvia got married and had a son? Could that son claim the throne he'd stolen from Numitor? And there was something else – an oracle. He'd received a prophecy he would be killed by a descendent of Numitor. He'd gotten Aegestes out of the way, and he didn't think Rhea Silvia would kill him. But she might have a son who would.

To prevent that, Amulius forced his niece to become a vestal virgin – a priestess of the goddess Vesta. The vestals pledged virginity for 30 years; if they had sexual relations with a man, they were stoned to death or buried alive, and any man that dishonored a vestal was beaten to death. Now, Silvia Rhea would remain childless, and Numitor would have no descendants to challenge Amulius' throne or kill him. Or would he?

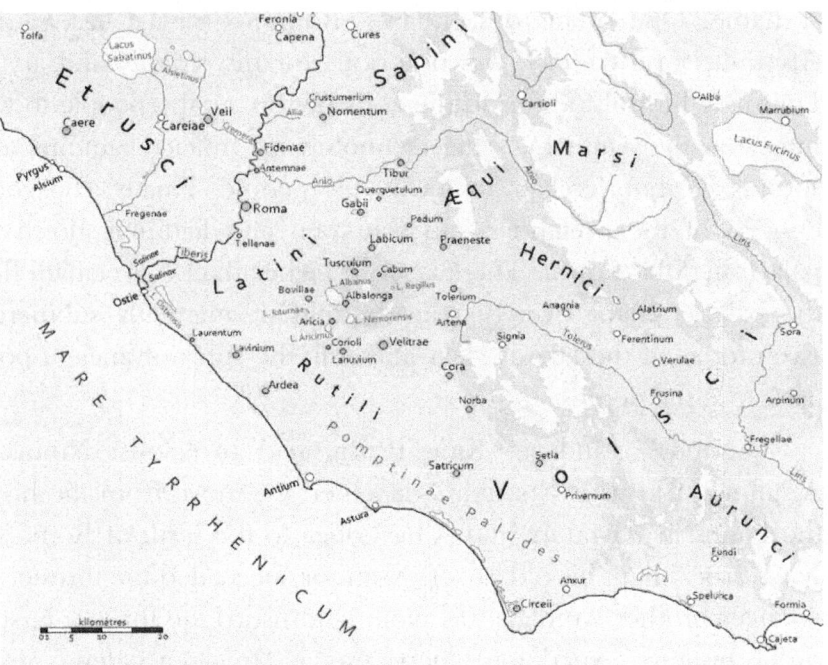

Map of Latin League cities and towns. To the north, on the coast, is the Etruscan (Estruci) nation, long-time enemies of the Latins. To the south, on the coast, is the Rutulian nation (Rutili), who, led by Turnus, fought with the Latins against the Trojans but were defeated. South of Rutili is the Volsci (the tribe of the woman warrior Camilla), who allied with the Latins but later were fierce enemies of Rome. Alba Longa is on the lake northeast of Rutili,

and Laurentum and Lavinium are nearer the coast. The towns surrounding Alba Longa – Lanuvium, Aricia, Bovillae, Tusculum, Tiber (to north on the river), Cora (to south), and Ardea on the coast – were some of the 30 towns and cities that joined the Latin League.

By Cassius Ahenobarbus - Own work, CC BY-SA 3.0, https://commons.wikimedia.org/w/index.php?curid=26875434

For now, let's explore the Latin Confederation or Latin League. During the 500 years that Aeneas's descendants ruled the Latins and Trojans, they formed the Latin League, probably in the seventh century BC. The Latin League was a confederation of about 30 cities and towns in the region of Latium, Lavinium, and Alba Longa. Most towns belonged to the Latin tribes or Latin-Trojans but included Cora and Pometia, which Livy said were Volscian towns, and Ardea, which is described in the Aeneid as the capital of the Rutuli.

The Latin League was a multi-ethnic, multi-tribal confederation formed for mutual defense against their common enemies – mostly the Etruscans. The leading city of the Latin League was Alba Longa, which would host annual celebrations for all the towns and cities to gather to worship Jupiter and feast together, which created a strong bond between the cities.

The Latin League also held conferences at the sacred grove of the goddess Ferentina, at the springs in the scenic valley between Lake Albano (where Alba Longa lay) and Marino. The tribes would assemble to resolve disputes between league members, deal with common problems that arose, and strategize against their enemies.

When Rome was just a fledgling city, it allied with the Latin League, still led by Alba Longa. These relations became shaky as Rome surged in power, a growing threat to the Latins. Around 534 BC, Tarquinius Superbus, the last king of Rome, called the Latin leaders together to persuade them to renew the alliance between the Latin League and Rome.

However, Turnus Herdonius, a leading Latin citizen and stateman, warned the League not to trust Tarquinius. To get rid of him, Tarquinius bribed Turnus' servant to stockpile swords in Turnus' tent and then charged Turnus with staging a coup. When everyone saw the "proof" of the swords, they executed him by drowning. The meeting resumed, and the Latins agreed that their troops would unite as a military force with the Roman troops.

In 509 BC, the Romans revolted against their monarchy, sent King Tarquinius into exile, and began self-rule as a republic. The Latin League allied with the exiled King Tarquinius against Rome in the Battle of Lake Regillus. The Romans won the battle, and in 493 BC, Rome and the 30 Latin-League cities established a treaty (the *Foedus Cassianum*), stipulating peace between the two powers, a Roman-Latin troop coalition against common enemies, and a two-way split of plunder from battles they fought together. Roman generals would command joint military campaigns.

Together, the Latin League and Roman coalition repelled the Aequi and Volsci tribes of the Apennine Mountains, defeated the Etruscans, and deflected the Celts invading from Gaul. However, the Latins and Romans often quarreled, mostly disputing over the spoils of joint battles. Rome combatted individual Latin cities and sometimes even the entire Latin League. The Latin cities felt increasingly threatened by Rome's soaring power.

The Latin War broke out in 343 BC between the Latins and Rome. Rome won the victory, dissolving the Latin League in 338 BC. The Latin cities came under the full control of Rome as colonies of the Roman Republic. The Latin people were considered Roman citizens but without voting rights. But all of that was still in the future. For now, we will return to Silva Rhea, priestess of Vesta, and discover what happened to her babies.

Chapter 3: From the Founding of Rome to the Last King

The vestal virgin – Princess Rhea Silvia – was pregnant. By whom? The story was she'd gone out to draw water, and in the momentary darkness of a solar eclipse, was raped by the god Mars. Her uncle, King Amulius, ordered his servant to kill the babies, remembering an oracle: he would be killed by his brother's descendent. And so, the infants were floated in a basket down the river Tiber.

Romulus and Remus were suckled by a wolf.
https://commons.wikimedia.org/wiki/File:Maison_de_la_Louve_(DSC_0377).jpg

Eventually, the basket bumped against the shore, and a she-wolf heard their cries. Her pups had died, and her teats were painfully swollen with milk. Lifting the babies from their basket, she nursed them. A shepherd named Faustulus came across this bizarre scene. As the wolf slunk into the underbrush, he scooped up the babies and carried them to his wife, who had just lost her own baby. She took them to her breast and raised them.

Romulus and Remus grew up unaware of their royal origins, tending flocks with their foster father. One day, they got into a conflict and killed some of Numitor's shepherds. Numitor arrested Remus, and Romulus rushed to tell Faustulus. Faustulus came to Numitor and told him the peculiar story of finding the twin boys with the wolf by the riverbank 18 years before. Numitor realized the twin boys had been found shortly after his daughter had given birth. These must be his grandsons!

After an emotional reunion with his long-lost grandsons, Numitor related how his ruthless brother Amulius had usurped the throne. The boys killed Amulius, fulfilling the prophecy, and restored their grandfather to his throne. Then, Romulus and Remus traveled back to the seven hills, about 12 miles north, planning to build their city where Faustulus had found them as infants. But they disagreed about where to build and who would be the ultimate sovereign. In a rage, Romulus killed his twin brother.

Romulus built the city on the Palatine Hill, beginning with fortifications. With only a small group of followers, he welcomed everyone from the surrounding regions to be citizens of the new city – including former slaves and those from the lower classes.

Settlements already existed in the seven hills area. Dionysius, Virgil, and Ovid all recorded that Evander of Arcadia (who had allied with Aeneas against Turnus) led his fellow Greeks to found the city of Pallantium centuries earlier, bringing the Greek gods, laws, and alphabet to Italy. Virgil said the Roman citizens were a mixture of Latins and Trojans from Alba Longa with Greeks from

Pallantium. The Sabines and Etruscans also lived in the immediate area; the Etruscans were an especially powerful people that at one time were the overlords of the Latins and Trojans until Ascanius had overthrown them and made them a tributary to Alba Longa.

After Romulus called a council to determine their government, the citizens put Romulus at the helm with a 100-person Senate. A *gen (clan)* was an extended-family group led by a *pater* (father) – the patriarch of the clan. The first senators were the *patres* – or family leaders of the gens. The descendants of these patres became the patrician class that formed the Senate.

What did the Senate do? Their key responsibility was electing new kings. When a king died, the Senate became the temporary ruling power while a new king was nominated and elected. The second most important task was serving as the king's advisory council. The Senate also served as a legislative body representing Rome's people. The king was the only one who could make laws, but he did so in close consultation with the Senate.

When Romulus first founded Rome, he had a problem – a shortage of women. Rome had about 3000 unmarried men who needed wives to sustain the new city. His new city was scorned by its neighbors, who refused to offer their daughters as wives to Rome's citizens. Romulus decided on another tactic to gain wives for his men.

The Romans abduct the Sabine women to be their wives. Painting by Nicolas Poussin.
https://commons.wikimedia.org/wiki/File:The_Abduction_of_the_Sabine_Women.jpg

The Romans invited the neighboring Sabine tribe to celebrate a religious festival with them. At the feast, the Romans drank diluted wine but gave the Sabine men full-strength liquor. The Romans pretended to get inebriated, and then when the Sabines had drunk themselves under the table, the Romans captured all the unmarried female guests to be their wives. When the Sabines sobered up and demanded their young women be returned, Romulus refused.

Outraged, two Sabine towns attacked almost immediately, attempting to recapture their young women, but the Romans defeated them. Finally, the Sabines mustered a united force led by King Tatius and attacked Rome. As the Romans and Sabines were drawn up in two opposing forces, the Sabine women, many pregnant by this point, ran into the space between the armies, shouting to the Sabines, "Why do you do this, fathers? Why do you do this, brothers?"

They then turned to the Romans, "Why do you do this, husbands? When will you stop fighting?"

Turning back to the Sabines, the women cried, "Spare your grandchildren! If not, then kill us since we're the reason you're fighting!"

Deeply moved, the warriors on both sides broke down weeping, put away their weapons, and held a peace conference. They joined into a united kingdom, with both Romulus and Tatius serving as co-rulers. King Tatius was mysteriously assassinated in Lavinium five years later, making Romulus the sole king of both the Latins and Sabines.

Rome also warred with the Etruscans, ancient enemies of the Latins and exiled Trojans. During Romulus' reign, the Fidenates, an Etruscan clan, attempted to obliterate Rome, considering it a future threat. Romulus marched out to their city, but rather than confront them directly, he set an ambush – hiding most of his men in the thickets while sending a small company of soldiers to the city gates to lure the Etruscans out. When the Fidenates stormed out in pursuit, the Romans leaped out, catching them by surprise and vanquishing them.

This worried the Etruscan citizens of nearby Veii. They launched a preemptive strike into Roman territory and quickly hurried home with their spoils of war. But Romulus led his men in hot pursuit, catching up with the Veientes just as they got back to their city. Rather than besieging the city, they ravaged their lands until the Veientes surrendered, made a 100-year peace treaty, gave Rome some of their lands.

When Rome's third king Tullus reigned, the Fidenates and Veientes launched a coordinated attack on Rome. By this point, Rome had joined the Latin League, so King Tullus called on King Mettius of Alba Longa to ally with him. Mettius and the Alban army arrived, unwillingly and slowly, but the Etruscans fled, nevertheless.

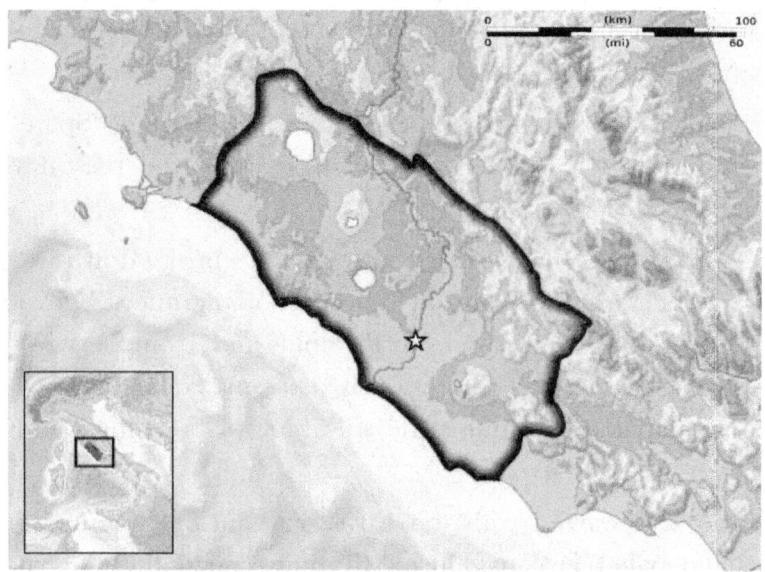

This map depicts the expansion of Roman territory in the late Roman monarchy period.
https://commons.wikimedia.org/wiki/File:Late_Roman_kingdom_map-blank.svg

Romulus and his descendants expanded Rome's borders by first allying with the Latin League to conquer common enemies, such as the Etruscans, then later conquering the Latin League, subjugating Latin cities to Rome. By kidnapping the Sabine women, they merged with the Sabine people in a joint rule. Gradually, Rome expanded its power base through central Italy.

Romulus was an astute warrior – but a poor politician. He was harsh and tyrannical with the Senate and haughty with his citizens. Dio recorded that the exasperated senators grew so incensed that they exploded in a frenzy, tearing him limb from limb. Just at that moment, a solar eclipse (like during his conception) and a violent windstorm occurred. The senators quickly hid the body and spread the tale that the windstorm had carried him away.

While the citizens were frantically searching for Romulus, his killers in the senate were in a quandary. They couldn't elect a new king unless Romulus was dead, but they didn't want to reveal their guilt. Finally, one senator rushed into the midst of the people, crying, "Don't grieve! I just saw Romulus ascending into the sky! He's become the god Quirinus. He said to elect a new king without delay."

Everyone believed him and stopped worrying about Romulus. They built a temple for him and moved on to who would be their next king.

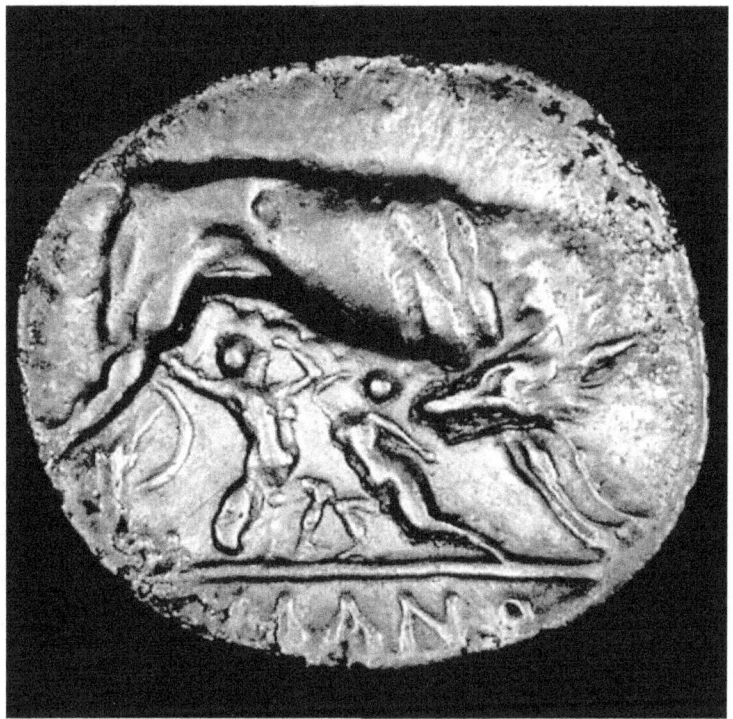

This silver didrachm Roman coin, dating to 269 BC, depicts the she-wolf suckling Romulus and Remus.
https://commons.wikimedia.org/wiki/File:Cr_20-1-Reverse.jpg

Was Romulus a real person? The Roman historian Marcus Terentius Varro (first century BC) said his tomb was located under the Forum. In November 2019, archeologists unearthed a sixth-century tomb beneath the steps of the Curia in the northwest corner of the Forum with a votive altar believed to be dedicated to Romulus. The stone sarcophagus is empty, but they didn't exactly have a body to bury – he was either torn to pieces or ascended bodily into the sky. Along with the bronze Capitoline Wolf sculpture in Rome that dates to the fifth century BC, numerous Roman coins dating to at least 269 BC show the she-wolf suckling the twins.

The Roman king was not hereditary but elected for life (or until he suddenly became a god). Now that Romulus was gone, the Sabines reminded everyone that a Sabine king was supposed to co-rule with a Roman king, and since King Tatius had been assassinated decades earlier and never replaced, it was their turn for a Sabine to rule over Rome. The Romans argued about this with the Sabines for a full year. With no king to rule, the Senate stepped in during this gap year (the *interregnum*), and each of the most distinguished senators ruled for five days in rotation.

Finally, the Sabines got their way, and Numa Pompilius was elected. He brought law and order to Rome and secured peace with the surrounding states. He lived a disciplined and simple life with few luxuries. Numa is known for implementing a 12-month calendar and naming January as the first month – after Janus, the god with two faces – one representing the past and the other the future.

The next king was Tullus Hostilius, a violent man of war who sneered at the gods. During his reign, he marched against Alba Longa, the mother city of Rome, but neither side wanted a long war against their kinsmen. After negotiations, they agreed to come under a common leadership – but who would lead? Alba Longa or Rome?

To decide, they held a small battle. Each side had a set of triplets who became the champions for the two sides – three against three. They battled each other until all three of the Albans were wounded and two of the Romans were dead. The surviving Roman, Horatius, didn't like the odds of three to one, so he ran away from the battleground, with the Albans chasing him, spreading out as they ran, slowed by their injuries. One by one, he turned and quickly killed the first, the second, and then the third, making Rome the ruler of Alba Longa.

Although the Albans were now allied with Rome, they feigned obedience to their overlords. Later, when King Tullus called them to help fight the Etruscans, they hung back, intending to fight with the Etruscans against Rome. Rome won the battle anyway, but Tullus executed their king, Mettius, and demolished Alba Longa for their duplicity.

Another Sabine, Ancus Marcius, was elected as Rome's fourth king. Like his grandfather, King Numa, he was peaceable but realized he was forced to engage in what he called "war as a means of peace." He fought against the Latins who were pillaging the Roman settlements, capturing their cities, and resettling many in Rome. He laid siege to the Etruscan Fidenates, long-time enemies of Rome, and subdued the Sabines. Marcius built the first bridge over the river Tiber and extended Rome's territory to the sea, giving them a port.

The fifth king of Rome, Lucius Tarquinius Priscus, was an outsider. His father was an exile from Corinth who had settled in Tarquinii, an Etruscan city, and married an Etruscan woman. Tarquinius grew up with great wealth, but being half-Greek, his political ambitions in Tarquinii went unrealized. He headed to Rome, hoping for a more promising future.

In Rome, his generosity, intelligence, and versatility won the admiration of influential people, especially King Marcius. Tarquinius would readily offer to help anyone needing assistance, never said or did anything unkind, and was quick to forgive others. Marcius was so impressed that he enrolled Tarquinius as a patrician, made him a senator, trusted him with the supervision of his children, and made him second in the kingdom. Through his cleverness and reputation of wisdom and honor, Tarquinius dominated Marcius and the senators.

When King Marcius died, the senators were planning to elect one (or both) of Marcius' sons to the throne. Tarquinius suggested himself as the temporary monarch until Marcius' sons came of age. He was so well-liked that virtually everyone agreed this was a splendid idea.

Tarquinius built the Circus Maximus for racing horses and chariots, gladiator confrontations, and games.

https://commons.wikimedia.org/wiki/File:CircusMaximusS%C3%BCdtrib%C3%BCne.JPG

Tarquinius expanded Rome's territory through the successful conquest of the Latins, Etruscans, and Sabines. He celebrated his military triumphs by riding in a golden chariot wearing a purple toga with gold embroidery and a crown of gold with precious stones. These persevered as symbols of Roman kings and emperors. He built the great stadium known as the *Circus Maximus* for games, chariot racing, and gladiator fights. He drained the marshy low-lying areas of Rome and provided waste removal with one of the world's first sewer systems – the *Cloaca Maxima.*

Tarquinius was a successful king, but the two sons of Marcius, who never received the promised crown, were plotting against him. Tarquinius made Servius Tullius (probably his illegitimate son) second-in-command and promoted him as his heir, which wasn't well-received: Tullius was the son of a slave – not of the patrician class. The sons of Marcius conspired with some patricians and sent two men into the palace who murdered Tarquinius with axes and sickles.

The paternity of the sixth Roman king, Servius Tullius, was a mystery. His mother was Ocrisia, a Latin slave-woman to Tarquinius' wife, Tanaquil. One story was that a man rose from the hearth flames as Ocrisia was offering sacrifices of food and wine. Frightened, Ocrisia ran to her mistress, and Queen Tanaquil, deciding he must be a god, dressed Ocrisia in wedding finery, sent her back into the room, and shut the door. Ocrisia conceived, and Tullius' half-god identity occasionally manifested by fire leaping from his head. The more probable story was that he was Tarquinius' illegitimate son since the king elevated him so highly, promoting him as his heir.

And now we come to Tullius' bizarre accession to the throne. Tarquinius had been assassinated, but Queen Tanaquil schemed to retain power by pretending he was still alive. She called to the people from the palace balcony, "My husband survived the attack! You'll see him shortly. He asks that Tullius take over his affairs while he is healing."

The citizens believed their queen, and Tullius took over as if he were receiving orders from Tarquinius. The murderers were arrested, executed, and Queen Tanaquil pretended to be tending to her husband, having agreed with Tullius he would be regent until her sons came of age. Fearful of being implicated in Tarquinius' assassination, King Marcius' sons fled to the Volsci kingdom.

With no other serious contenders for the throne, Tullius and Tanaquil revealed the sad news that Tarquinius had succumbed to his wounds. Tullius continued as the regent while Tarquinius' sons were growing up. He groomed the citizens to accept him as king – assigning them land (so they could vote – for him, of course). He also planned to free the slaves and give them citizenship, perhaps because his mother was a slave.

This last plan incensed the patricians. Not only would they lose labor, but the freed slaves would support Tullius. They circulated charges that Tullius was ruling without the Senate's sanction. Tullius gathered the people and gave a stirring oration of all the reasons he was their best choice for king. Immediately, the citizens of Rome voted him in as their monarch.

Tullius took the first census of Rome, which had about 80,000 citizens. He gave his daughters in marriage to the two sons of Tarquinius, still promising to restore the monarchy to them when the time was right. The oldest son, Tarquin, realizing his father-in-law would never relinquish the throne, plotted a takeover. When his younger brother refused to cooperate, he gave poison to his sister-in-law to kill him. When his wife criticized his plot, he poisoned her as well, then married his sister-in-law. His new wife happily plotted with him against her father.

Lucius gathered a group of patricians and senators unhappy with King Tullius, lauding the stellar leadership of his father Tarquinius while ridiculing Tullius. Hearing of this, Tullius hurried to the Senate but only blurted out a few words before Tarquin forced him out of the building, throwing him down the stairs. The bewildered king sat on the pavement, amazed that no one came to assist him.

After congratulating her husband on his successful coup d'état, Tullia ran her chariot over her father's body. Painting by Jean Bardin. https://commons.wikimedia.org/wiki/File:Bardin_Tullia.jpg

The Senate took an immediate vote to elect Tarquin as their king. His first act was ordering the death of Tullius, who was stumbling home, abandoned by his guards. Tarquin's wife congratulated her husband with an embrace, saluted him as her king, then charged off in her chariot, driving over the body of her father as he lay in the street.

When Lucius Tarquinius Superbus succeeded to the throne, he surrounded himself with bodyguards, fearful of what had happened to his father. Desiring to rid himself of any senators who would question the murder of Tullius or his right to the throne, he decimated their numbers: executing those against whom he could bring plausible charges, secretly murdering some, and banishing others.

He didn't stop with Tullius' followers; he even killed his close friends who had conspired with him, fearful they would turn against him later. He didn't appoint new senators to replace the dead ones, desiring to render the Senate powerless. He ran the state's affairs with only his sons to assist him, not wanting anyone else to rise in power. He was inaccessible to both citizens and senators, displaying shocking brutality and arrogance. Besides killing his brother and first wife, Tarquin also killed his sister's husband and son. The second son of Tarquin's sister, Lucius Junius Brutus, feigned intellectual disability to survive.

Tarquin expanded Rome's borders and power through canny negotiations with the Latins, triumphant conquest of the Volsci, and subterfuge with the city of Gabii. He achieved peace with the Aequi and renewed Rome's treaty with the Etruscans and Sabines. He also continued his father's construction projects on the stadium and the sewers.

Tarquin's downfall came from a coup d'état led by his nephew Brutus, the one who pretended to be cognitively challenged. It all started when Tarquin's son Sextus raped Lucretia, the beautiful wife of a distinguished senator. Afterward, Lucretia told her husband

and father what had happened, asking them to avenge her, then pulled a dagger from under her pillow and killed herself.

This spurred an uproar against the tyrannical rule of the Tarquin family. Brutus persuaded the military to join him in the revolt. King Tarquin and his sons fled Rome, where he rallied some Etruscan and Latin cities to his support and attempted to retake Rome three times, but he lost and died in exile. After Tarquin was deposed, the citizens of Rome established the Roman Republic in 509 BC, with magistrates elected each year, representative assemblies, separation of powers, and a constitution that mandated a system of checks and balances.

PART TWO:
THE ROMAN REPUBLIC
(509 to 27 BC)

Chapter 4: The Republic's Establishment

The Roman Republic, lasting five centuries, led Rome's stunning metamorphosis from a modest city-state to a far-reaching domain stretching around the Mediterranean. The Romans had an incredible ability to assimilate organizational methods, knowledge, and technique from other powers they encountered and put that into play as their borders swiftly extended and their governmental system evolved.

The Roman Republic left an impressive legacy that markedly influenced the organization of new governments around the world – like the United States – two millennia later. Officially called the *Senate and People of Rome (Senatus Populusque Romanus),* the Republic ushered in a rule of the people in 509 BC when they expelled the tyrannical King Tarquinius Superbus. The Romans realized they didn't need a king – they would run things on their own. And they did, until 27 BC when Octavian (Augustus Caesar) became the first Roman emperor.

This involved a learning curve; they had to figure out just how to run a republic because that hadn't been done before – by anybody. Greece was working out something called a democracy, but their system was different; the Greek ideal was the rule of the many (regular people) over the few (rich aristocrats), and the Roman Republic, at least initially, was the rule of the elite Patricians over the Plebeian masses of common people.

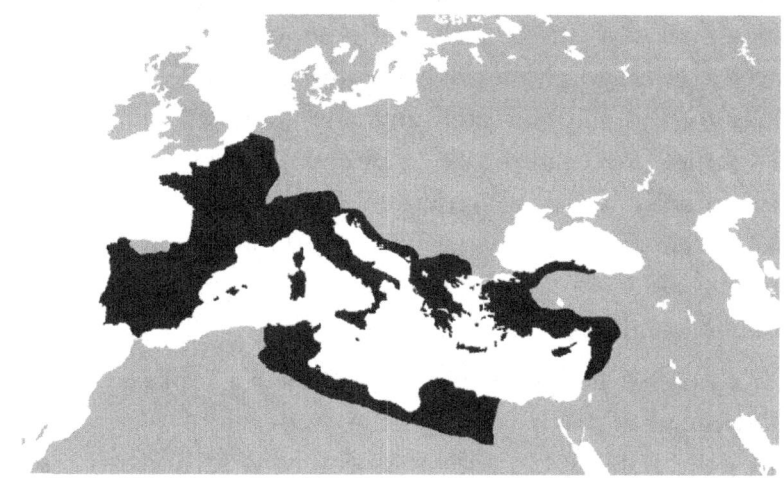

This map shows the extent of the areas conquered by Rome by 44 BC - close to the end of the Republic era. In this map, the seas are white - so you can see how much of the Mediterranean Sea (in the middle) was controlled by Rome.
https://commons.wikimedia.org/wiki/File:Roman_Republic-44BC.png

The Romans had to employ a great deal of ingenuity and flexibility - just when they thought they had the republican system mastered, something would happen. What should they do with all these people they were conquering. How would the Republic form of government work for them? And, what about these Plebeian commoners having the audacity to demand equal representation? As if that weren't enough, the slaves revolted! The Roman Republic was constantly evolving and adapting to one crisis after another.

Their biggest challenge was the internal conflict that had cursed Rome from the day Romulus murdered his twin brother. The wealth and power Rome was accumulating did not mitigate the destructive discord that spelled the collapse of Rome's Republic.

But to their credit, they held it together spectacularly for five centuries, all the while conquering much of the known world.

The rape of virtuous Lucretia sparked a revolution, overturning the monarchy that had ruled Rome since its inception. The ensuing constitutional reforms launched Rome into a new era with a stronger constitution. They'd had unwritten guidelines – and the constitution was still unwritten, but now they had innovations like term limits, separation of powers, checks and balances, impeachments, quorum requirements, filibusters, vetoes, and regularly scheduled elections. The constitution was continuously evolving, based on precedent, and driven by conflict between commoners and aristocrats.

Two men serving together – called consuls – replaced the former kings. Instead of serving for life, they were elected for a one-year term by the military Centuriate Assembly. The Romans reasoned that two heads of state were better than one because if one made disastrous decisions, the other could use his veto power to keep him in check. A consul could be prosecuted at the end of his one-year term if he abused his powers.

The two consuls wore white togas with a broad purple border, indicating their position and power to command as the highest judicial power in the Republic. The consuls appointed new senators (during the early Republic) and exercised supreme authority in military and civil affairs. One led the Centuriate Assembly, and the other led the Assembly of Tribes. When on military campaigns, they would each command an army with nearly absolute power.

The idea of having two men lead the country assisted by a Senate was quickly picked up by Carthage in North Africa. After becoming a Republic in 509 BC, Rome established a treaty with Carthage, which controlled North Africa and the Western Mediterranean with its powerful navy. Like Rome, Carthage established a Senate of 300 affluent citizens with two heads of state they called *Suffetes* or judges.

"The Oath of Brutus," by François-Joseph Navez, depicts Brutus' vow to avenge Lucretia.

https://commons.wikimedia.org/wiki/File:Fran%C3%A7ois-Joseph_Navez001.jpg

The first two consuls of the Roman Republic were Lucius Junius Brutus and Lucius Tarquinius Collatinus, the revolutionaries who overthrew the monarchy. Brutus was the grandson of King Lucius Tarquinius Priscus and the nephew of Rome's last king, Tarquinius Superbus. The men carried Lucretia's body to the Forum, where Brutus shouted, "Act like men and Romans and take up arms against our insolent foes!"

Brutus was the one who'd been pretending to be mentally deficient so his uncle – the king – wouldn't kill him. Now he had to explain to the crowd he had faked disability because his evil uncle had killed his father and brother. He proposed banishing the king and forming a republic form of government. Moved by the sight of Lucretia's bloody body, a vote was taken: the king was out, and the Republic was in.

The other first consul, Lucius Tarquinius Collatinus, was Lucretia's husband, the nephew of King Lucius Tarquinius Priscus. He was a cousin of both Brutus and Sextus Tarquinius, his wife's rapist. Ironically, these two men who instigated the revolt and served as the first consuls belonged to the royal family they overthrew. When the dust settled, the people murmured about Collatinus' connection to the Tarquin tyrants, so he abdicated his position as consul.

Oddly enough, though more closely related to the former royal family than Collatinus, Brutus did not receive such suspicion, perhaps because he resolutely executed his own two sons when he discovered they were part of a conspiracy to restore Tarquin as king. Brutus died before the end of his one-year term when he and his first cousin Arruns (son of Tarquin) killed each other at the Battle of Silva Arsia.

In emergencies – such as a military or internal crisis – one consul could nominate a temporary dictator, following the Senate's recommendation, who would be confirmed by the Comitia Curiata. The dictator was expected to relinquish his powers once the crisis was abated – or at the end of six months – whichever came first. In the later years of the Republic, the Plebs gained the power to nullify the dictator's executive actions, which reduced his power to act swiftly in times of crisis; by 202 BC, this position was no longer utilized.

Under the consuls were the censors and the praetors. The censors oversaw the census and maintained public morality (from which we get the English word *censor* for an official who suppresses any behaviors, communications, or objects considered obscene, politically unacceptable, or a threat to security).

Marcus Claudius Marcellus was elected as consul five times and celebrated for killing King Viridomarus, commander of the Gauls, in hand-to-hand combat in 222 BC.

https://commons.wikimedia.org/wiki/File:Print_Marcus_Claudius_Marcellus_Roman_Consul_Elect_Statue_Spolia_Opima_Rome.jpg

Rome's elected praetors served as judges of Roman law and as army generals. As Rome conquered more territory, the praetors served as governors of the provinces. When the two consuls were away on military campaigns, the Praetor Urbanus became the senior official over the city of Rome. He couldn't leave Rome if the consuls were not there, except for very brief periods. He could call the Senate together and command a defense if the city were attacked. Each year, the Praetor Urbanus issued an Edict that legislated the rights and dues of people.

The people living in Rome during the Republic era weren't automatically citizens – and even if they were, there were distinct levels of citizenship. People over 15 who descended from the original 35 tribes of Rome had the right of citizenship – unless they were a slave, a former slave, or a woman. Women could own property, run a business, and get a divorce, but they couldn't vote or hold a position in government. Slaves weren't even considered people. Freedmen (former slaves) eventually won limited citizenship. The tribes of Rome weren't ethnic or family groups but based on geographic location – something like a congressional district.

Men with full citizenship with all the accompanying political and legal rights proudly wore white togas to display their status as *Optimo Jure* (optimum rights). Each full citizen belonged to one of the three voting or legislative assemblies. During the monarchy period, Romans had only one voting assembly – the *Comitia Curiata* (Curiate Assembly) – but most of the political powers of this assembly were transferred to the Comitia Centuriata (Assembly of Centuries) for the military men and the Comitia Tributa (Tribal Assembly) for those of the patrician ruling class. These assemblies were each led by one of the two consuls. In 494 BC, the Concilium Plebis (Plebeian Assembly) was organized for the common people (called Plebs or Plebeians).

Each citizen had the right to elect the leaders of their respective assemblies. Their assembly leaders elected the magistrates, passed laws, and held capital trials. The military assembly (Centuriate Assembly) was the only power that could declare war and ratify a census. It also served as a Supreme Court of Appeals for certain cases.

The tribunes filled several offices, most notably the *Tribuni Plebis* and the *Tribuni Militum*. The Tribuni Plebis, which numbered from two to ten elected tribunes, presided over the Plebeian Assembly, organizing legislation for the vote and vetoing legislation from the Senate that disfavored the common people. Using the commoners as a political weapon, the Tribuni Plebis exercised great control over Rome.

The Military Tribunes took care of organizing command among the ranks, supervising logistics, and leading legions to battle. They had senior rank in the Roman army and had to serve for at least five years. Other tribunes included the *Tribuni Aerarii,* who served in the treasury, collecting taxes and distributing the funds – mostly to the Roman legions.

The magistrates were elected officials with extensive authority in the public sphere and the military. The two consuls were the lead magistrates, and the most influential aristocratic families (*gentes)* dominated the most powerful magistrate positions. Each magistrate had a *provincia* – a scope of authority over a geographic region or a specific responsibility. The Patricians – and later the Plebeians – voted for their magistrates, so it was a form of representation by the people. Magistrates maintained the peace and could sentence people for crimes with the power of *coercitio* (coercion). They were also supposed to keep an eye out for omens, which the Romans took seriously.

Just like they had two consuls in top leadership, most of the magisterial offices had two people for the same position – called the *Collega* (collegiality) – which checked abuse of power. Roman citizens were protected from abuse of the coercion power through *provocation* (due process). Magistrates served one-year terms and had to wait ten years before they could hold that office again.

The Senate continued into the Republic but in a different capacity. In the Republic, the Senate's main responsibilities were electing new kings and advising the king. In the Republic, the Senate passed *Senatus Consulta* to the magistrates, which meant *senator's advice*, but the magistrates followed it as more of a decree. The Senate placed most of their focus on foreign policy, particularly as they were constantly adding in new provinces throughout Italy and eventually around the Mediterranean. The Senate also had explicit power over the state budget, which translated to power over the military and many other entities. The Senate's influence grew immensely over time and began passing laws as the legislative assemblies' strength faded.

In the early years of the Republic, the Senators were appointed by the two consuls, and of course, they selected men who would support them politically. Around 312 BC, the Plebeian Assembly successfully gave the Roman censors the power to appoint the new senators (for life) from a pool of newly-elected magistrates, bringing the Senate out from under the power of the consuls. In emergencies – war or civil unrest – the new senators were selected by the temporary dictator or by the current senators.

The Via Appia, (Apian Way) Rome's first major road, was built 312-264 BC and stretched 150 miles from Rome to Benevento.
Photo by Paul Vlaar. Original uploader was Neep at en.wikipedia. Later versions (crop) were made and uploaded by Ali'i at en.wikipedia. - CC BY-SA 3.0, https://commons.wikimedia.org/w/index.php?curid=8767120

At the beginning of the Republic, the Senate had 100 men. After 312 BC, when the censors got to appoint senators, Appius Claudius Caecus raised the number of senators to 300 and included Plebs and descendants of freed slaves, which the Patricians considered a scandalous plummet into the abyss. During his one-year term as censor, Caecus launched the construction of the Aqua Appia - the first Roman aqueduct - and the Apian Way - the first major Roman road, traveling 150 miles from Rome to Benevento in the south. As the Roman Republic was nearing its end, the number of senators increased to 900 under Sulla and 1000 under Julius Caesar.

Rome had three classes of people. At the bottom were slaves, who had no power or representation in government. At the top were the Patricians – wealthy, upper-class citizens from noble families, who were successful businessmen or large landholders. The Plebeians were everyone else – the working class.

In the early years of the Republic, the Patricians dominated politics and society, monopolizing the priesthood, important military posts, and prestigious magistracies. The original Patricians were an exclusive group of 50 distinguished extended families called *gentes,* of whom the most eminent was the Cornelii gens. Other esteemed gentes of the Republic era included the Aemilii, Valerii, Fabii, and Claudii families – recognized for their massive landholdings, wealth, and patronage of their *clients.* Clients were usually commoners for whom the Patrician patrons took responsibility: providing legal representation in court, financial assistance, marriage arrangements, and other favors.

The Plebeians or Plebs formed the backbone of Rome: the farmers, artisans, merchants, and other workers. Initially, they had little political power. Their influence quickly grew as they developed an internal social organization and legislative assembly, passing their own laws and holding the power of veto over the Senate.

Higher positions in the priesthood and politics were off-limits to Plebians. One grievance of the Plebs was that the Patricians would pass laws, not inform the Plebs, and then prosecute them for breaking laws they didn't know existed. Another grievance was beating and imprisoning debtors unable to repay their debts.

If the Patricians got too outrageous, the Plebeians would go on strike in a *Secessio Plebis* (Plebeian withdrawal). They would close shop, put down their tools, and walk out of the city, heading to a nearby mountain to enjoy a little vacation time, leaving the Patricians to fend for themselves. After a few days with no shops to buy food or goods, no construction workers, no bodyguards, no soldiers, and none of the other services the Plebs provided, the Patricians were ready to come to the negotiating table.

Gaius Gracchus represented the Plebeians, advocating for great reforms until his suicide in 121 BC.
https://commons.wikimedia.org/wiki/File:Gaius_Gracchus_Tribune_of_the_People.jpg

Various strikes resulted in the easing of debt punishments, access to new laws, and acquiring their own legislative assembly and tribunes. Little by little, the Plebs achieved political equality with the upper classes. The tribunes safeguarded the Plebeians from abuse and could exercise *intercession,* or veto the Senate's laws and actions, and block any magistrate or even a fellow tribune failing to consider the Plebs' best interest. In the late Republic era, tribunes could be Senate members, which gave them great sway over legislation; they acquired a reputation of being revolutionaries within the system.

The veto (*intercessio*) was a powerful tool created by the Romans that still regulates many government systems today. Each of the two consuls could veto the actions of the other. The tribunes could veto the Senate's decrees or magistrates' actions, especially protecting the common citizens from unfair domination by the aristocracy. The Senate could still pass a bill, but it was impotent if vetoed.

In 385 BC, Marcus Manlius Capitolinus, who provided heroic defense for Rome amid the sacking of the Gauls, was troubled by the devastating effect the invasion had on the Plebs. Losing their livelihoods – their shops, farms, and tools – plunged them into nightmarish debt to the Patricians. Manlius watched as a centurion, who had defended Rome from the Gauls, was led to prison for debts he could not pay. Manlius suddenly leaped forward, offering to pay the man's debt himself, and the centurion walked home a free man.

A Patrician himself, Manlius became a champion for the Plebeian class, even selling off his estate to pay off their debts. He relentlessly advocated for the Plebs, charging the Senate with embezzling public funds that could relieve the horrific misery of the common workers who contributed so much to the city. His efforts at social reform were not well received by the Patricians, who threw him to his death from the Tarpeian Rock.

The menacing unrest continued in rollercoaster fashion between the Patricians and Plebs: the Plebs made gains and then lost them again as their rights were suppressed. In 366 BC, Dictator Camillus resolved the crisis by a compromise – the Plebians got their own consul, while the Patricians had a monopoly over the offices of praetor and *curule aediles* (formal magistrates). Once they got their own censor, it wasn't long before the positions of censor and dictator were filled by Plebs. Gaius Marcius Rutilus, a Plebeian, served as consul four times, then dictator, and finally as censor.

As the Plebeians accomplished striking advances in politics and society, they were experiencing an internal separation of classes. Some of the Plebs were becoming affluent elitists who, like the Patricians, were exploiting the poorer Plebs to their advantage. They had grown out of touch with the working class and were failing to represent their issues. The Patricians' loss of power led to many prominent gentes fading away, supplanted by the self-made new aristocrats – twenty families of Plebeians – joining the dozen or so remaining Patrician gentes to form the new class known as *Nobilitas*.

Chapter 5: The Wars of Central Italy

From the Republic's inception in 509 BC, Rome endured almost perpetual warfare. The first 200 years of conquest and defense solidified Roman power in central Italy and parts of southern Italy. The wars of this era began with the Tarquinian Conspiracy, then the Celtic invasion, and the Sack of Rome, followed by war with the Apennine Mountain Samnites. Throughout epic battles, the Romans demonstrated astounding resilience, overcoming catastrophic losses.

Tarquinius Superbus' insidious attempts to regain the throne swept the Romans, Etruscans, and Latins into the intrigue known as the Tarquinian Conspiracy. Having brazenly murdered his wife, brother, and father-in-law to gain the throne, Tarquinius was now seeking any means possible to recapture it. He began by sending ambassadors to the Senate requesting the return of the royal family's personal belongings. While the Senate was debating their request, Tarquin's ambassadors were secretly instigating a coup d'état, recruiting even Brutus' two sons and his wife's two brothers (of the Vitelii family) as chief conspirators, along with the Aquillii family.

These young men met at the Aquillii house, where Tarquin's ambassadors were staying, swearing a dreadful oath sealed by pouring out the blood of a man they'd killed and touching his entrails. A slave named Vindicius happened to walk into the darkened room, unnoticed by the others. Observing the horrific scene and hearing their plans to kill the two consuls, Vindicius stole out of the house and alerted the consuls. The conspirators were hustled to the Forum; because their letters to King Tarquin were discovered, their guilt was undisputed. Brutus called out to his sons, "Come, Titus, come Tiberius, why aren't you defending yourselves against these charges?"

Three times Brutus demanded an answer, but they remained silent. Brutus resolutely turned to the guards, "Do what you must do."

Brutus watched with an expression of stern wrath as his sons were seized, stripped of their togas, and beaten with rods. When they were thrown to the ground and beheaded, a groan escaped Brutus, stoic up to this point. He silently rose and walked out, leaving the rest of the conspirators to be judged and executed.

The guards return the bodies of Lucas' sons.
https://commons.wikimedia.org/wiki/File:David_Brutus.jpg

Unwilling to admit defeat, Tarquinius rallied the Etruscans of Veii and his ancestral city of Tarquinii, confronting Rome in the fierce Battle of Silva Arsia. His son, Arruns, and the Roman consul, Brutus, were killed when the cousins simultaneously impaled each other with their spears. Having lost that battle, Tarquinius next allied with Lars Porsena, the king of the powerful Etruscan city of Clusium.

In 508 BC, King Porsena marched on Rome, approaching the Pons Sublicius bridge over the Tiber. Three fearless young men – Horatius, Herminius, and Lartius – dashed across the bridge to valiantly hold off the Etruscans while the Romans frantically destroyed the bridge behind them. Herminius and Lartius ran back just as the bridge collapsed, while Horatius jumped off the bridge as it fell, swimming back under a hail of Etruscan arrows and spears.

King Porsena lay siege to Rome, blocked river transportation, and raided the surrounding farms. One night, an extraordinary young man named Gaius Mucius snuck into the Etruscan camp, intending to assassinate Porsena, but mistakenly killed the king's scribe instead. Captured, he boldly declared to King Porsena why he was there. "You'll never stop us! I'm only the first of 300 Roman youths who will do the same!"

Thrusting his hand into the flames of a nearby brazier, he cried, "Look! See how cheap our bodies are to men whose focus is great glory!"

Gaius confronts the Etruscan king Porsena after his failed assassination attempt.
https://upload.wikimedia.org/wikipedia/commons/0/0e/Matthias_Stomer_-_Mucius_Scaevola_in_the_presence_of_Lars_Porsenna_-_Google_Art_Project.jpg

Horrified yet admiring the young man's brazen courage, King Porsena released Gaius and sent his ambassadors to negotiate peace with Rome. The Romans staunchly refused his request for Tarquinius' restoration as king, yet they did return the land to the Veientes they had taken earlier. Shortly after, many Etruscans came to Rome to live and were granted their own district.

Around 496 BC, Tarquinius Superbus, leading the Latin League, waged the Battle of Lake Regillus against Rome in a last-ditch attempt to regain the crown. Rome appointed Aulus Postumius Albus as temporary dictator. The Volsci had allied with the Latins, but the Romans rushed out so quickly, enraged by the sight of their former king, they won the battle before the Volsci arrived.

In the 483 BC Fabian War, Veii took advantage of Rome's internal unrest and an invasion by the Aequi (a tribe to the east) and marched on Rome. Rome's Fabii clan asked and received permission to deal with the Veientes, and 309 soldiers of their gens marched north, demolishing the Veii territory. However, the Veientes ambushed and annihilated all the Fabii men. Rome sent a second army against the Veientes and lost once again. The following year, the Veientes allied with the Sabines against Rome. This time the Romans allied with the Latins and were triumphant, and a truce was declared with the Etruscans paying tribute to Rome.

The 458 BC Battle of Mount Algidus was fought against the Aequi, who attacked Rome's territories at an inopportune time: Rome's slaves were revolting, the Patricians and Plebs were deadlocked in toxic politics, and one of their consuls had just died. Despite their internal woes, Rome defeated the Aequi, but the following year the Aequi attacked again. Cincinnatus, nominated as a temporary dictator, vanquished the Aequi so swiftly that he was able to resign his dictatorship in only 16 days.

The Aequi and Volsci allied against Rome in the 446 BC Battle of Corbio, outnumbering the Roman forces. The Romans divided into two armies, taking on the Aequi-Volsci coalition from two sides. The Aequi retreated – technically a victory for Rome – but with at least 6000 Roman casualties. In a little over 60 years, the Roman Republic had gained ascendancy over their nearest neighbors – the Etruscans and Latins – and were preparing to deal with the threatening Apennine hill tribes when an unexpected foe suddenly invaded.

The Senones were a Gallic tribe of the Celtic people from the Seine basin in northern France. As their population grew, part of this tribe crossed the Alps, invading northern Italy and founding what is now Milan. In 387 BC, these Celtic people collided with Rome. The Senones had learned about central Italy's rich farmland from a young man named Aruns who lived in the Etruscan city of Clusium. When the king's son seduced his wife, the bitter Aruns left his city to sell wine, figs, and olives in northern Italy, where he encountered the Senones. The Gauls were fascinated with his products, and Aruns saw an avenue for revenge. He told them he came from a fertile land, sparsely populated with inept fighters. They could easily take the land for their own and enjoy this wine and food every day.

So, the Gauls marched on Clusium, who desperately asked Rome for aide. Rome sent three ambassadors – the Fabii brothers – who cautioned the Senone people not to attack Clusium unless they wanted to fight Rome. A scuffle broke out, and one ambassador killed a Senone chieftain, breaking the *Law of Nations* that ambassadors couldn't engage in violence.

The Senones sent ambassadors to Rome, demanding Rome hand over the three Fabii brothers in payment for their chieftain. The Senate didn't want to offend the Gauls, but the Fabii gens was so powerful that the three brothers had just been elected as military tribunes. Outraged, the Gallic ambassadors took word of this back to Clusium, and the Senones marched on Rome.

The Romans were thunderstruck when the Senones swiftly marched against them in the Battle of the Allia (around 387 BC), led by their Celtic chieftain Brennes. Rome was unprepared and outnumbered. Rome's army marched out, crossed the Tiber, and met the Celts about ten miles north of Rome.

The army positioned themselves with two flanks, with the most inexperienced warriors on the hill to the right flank. The Senone chieftain, Brennus, put his strongest men on the side facing the hill. When the two forces collided, the weaker Roman flank on the hill was pushed back, and the flank on the left was pinned against the river. The Gauls charged the sparse middle ranks of the Romans, dividing the army in two.

In a panic, both flanks of the Roman army retreated in a disorderly flight. The panic-stricken left flank attempted to swim across the river, but the inexperienced swimmers or those with heavy armor were drowned. The survivors fled to Veii as the remnants of the right flank fled back to Rome. At least half of the Roman army perished, while the Senones suffered few casualties.

The Celts were astonished by their swift, extraordinary victory. They spent two days looting the Roman camp and then set off for Rome. Reaching the city just before sunset, they were startled to see the city gates open and unarmed. Not wanting to battle at night in unfamiliar territory, they set up camp near Rome.

The men in Veii thought they were the only survivors and that Rome was lost. In the city, meanwhile, the people were in hysterics, thinking that most of their army had been wiped out. They didn't know part of their army was sheltering in Veii. The remnant of the army, any able-bodied men, and their leaders headed up the Capitoline Hill with weapons and food and as many valuables and sacred items as they could carry. Fencing off the hill, they hunkered down.

The common people grabbed what provisions they could, barricaded their houses and streets, and bolted. When the Gauls arrived two days later, most of the city had emptied. But many priests and the elderly men who had served as consuls stayed. Dressing in their ceremonial robes, they swept into the Forum and sat in their ivory chairs, waiting.

The Senone Gauls were amazed by the aged Roman priests and statesmen sitting stoically in their ivory chairs.
https://commons.wikimedia.org/wiki/File:The_story_of_Rome,_from_the_earliest_times_t o_the_death_of_Augustus,_told_to_boys_and_girls_(1912)_(14773070063).jpg

On the third day, the Senones arrived, entering the open gate tentatively, fearing an ambush. Finding no one around, they plundered the city. Arriving at the Forum, they found the ancient priests and former consuls in their magnificent robes, sitting majestically on their ivory thrones. The Gauls stood in reverence, not sure what to do, wondering if the men were gods. Finally, one stroked the beard of an aged Patrician, who indignantly smacked him on the head with his ivory staff. At that provocation, Gauls slaughtered the aged men in the Forum and anyone else they found in the city.

The Gauls looted and burned the city, destroying valuable documents of Roman history and holding Rome for seven months. They could not take the Capitoline Hill – it was so steep that the small force at the summit held them off. Meanwhile, the Roman soldiers who had fled to Veii were regrouping and stockpiling arms.

The Senones were raiding the surrounding countryside and towns for food and made the unfortunate mistake of raiding the farms near the town of Ardea. A former Roman dictator, Camillus, lived in Ardea, exiled by his political enemies. Learning that the Gauls were prone to getting drunk at night, Camillus and the men of Ardea attacked the Celtic camp at night, killing many men.

The Romans who had fled to towns and villages of the area asked Camillus to be their leader. He insisted it be official, so a young man snuck back to Rome, scaled the steepest part of the Capitoline Hill, and got approval from the senators for Camillus to be appointed dictator again. As official dictator, Camillus then mustered a 12,000-man army of the remaining Roman soldiers, the men of Ardea, and allies from Veii and other cities.

Back in Rome, the Senones noticed the places where rocks and plants had been torn away as the young Roman had scaled the Capitoline hill. That night, a group followed the same path up the hill, unheard by the sleeping guards at the top. But the sacred geese of Juno's temple on the summit awakened and charged the Gauls, honking, pecking, and flapping their wings. The clamor woke the Romans, who fended off the Senones.

The Romans on the Capitoline hill had run out of food. They were comforted to learn that part of the army was alive and well in Veii but had no idea how long it would be for Camillus to muster an army. The Senones were also in a bad way, surrounded by the corpses of the Romans they had killed but not buried, suffering from the heat, and decimated by malaria and dysentery. Their chieftain Brennus and the Roman military tribune Sulpicius met together; the Romans agreed to pay one thousand pounds in gold for the Gauls to immediately vacate the city and surrounding country.

When the Romans weighed out the gold, they felt cheated by the Senone's scale. With an evil laugh, Brennus stripped off his sword belt, and threw his sword and belt on the scale, adding to the weight. "Woe to the vanquished!" he smirked.

Just at that moment, Camillus arrived with his thousands of soldiers, marching right up to where the confrontation over the gold was taking place. Lifting the gold from the scales, he handed it to his attendants, then ordered the Gauls to take their scale and leave. "Rome will be delivered by iron, not gold!"

The Roman Consul Camillus confronts the Gallic Chieftain Brennus over the gold.
https://commons.wikimedia.org/wiki/File:Sebastiano_Ricci_-_Camillus_Rescuing_Rome_from_Brennus_-_27.537_-_Detroit_Institute_of_Arts.jpg

Brennus sputtered in outrage, but Camillus asserted the contract was not legally binding: as the elected dictator of Rome, it was made without his agreement. After a small skirmish, Brennus and his men abandoned Rome and camped about eight miles away. The following day, Camillus' army attacked; according to Livy, the Gauls were slaughtered, with not even a messenger to report the great massacre.

Samnite soldiers march to war, as depicted in a fourth century BC tomb frieze in Nola, Campania.
https://commons.wikimedia.org/wiki/File:Samnite_soldiers_from_a_tomb_frieze_in_Nola_4th_century_BCE.jpg

After rebuilding its city and population, Rome was embroiled in three wars with the Samnite tribe of the Apennine Mountains from 343 to 290 BC. The struggle for control of central and southern Italy also involved the Etruscans, Senones, Umbri, Picentes, and more. Rome ultimately defeated all the Etruscan and Latin tribes and consolidated dominion over the area.

The first war began when the Samnites attacked Campania, who asked Rome for help. The Campanians wanted a treaty, but Rome couldn't, as they already had a treaty with the Samnites. So, the Campanians surrendered, making themselves a possession of Rome. Rome then sent envoys to the Samnites, asking them not to harass Campania as this was now Roman territory. Defiantly, the

Samnites ordered their armies to immediately march against Campania and raze it. When further negotiations failed, Rome declared war on the Samnites and won three battles, ending the first war.

In 328 BC, Rome founded a settlement at Fregellae on the ruins of a Volsci town the Samnites had destroyed. The nearby Volscian towns of Fabrateria and Luca asked Rome to be their overlords in exchange for protection from the Samnites. This instigated the Second Samnite War. As tensions between the Samnites and Rome flared for several years, Rome assiduously formed alliances with the surrounding tribes, such as the Lucanians and the Apulians in the southernmost part of Italy. Meanwhile, the Samnites had allied with the Vestini.

In 321 BC, the Samnites spread the rumor they were preparing to attack the city of Lucera, a Roman ally. A Roman army quickly marched that way, taking the fastest route through the Caudine Forks in the Apennine Mountains, where they had to pass through a narrow ravine. Before they arrived, the Samnites blocked the furthest end of the ravine with tree trunks and boulders. Once the Romans entered the ravine, they blocked the other end, trapping the Roman army in the ravine.

Gaius, the Samnite commander, ordered the Romans to surrender, evacuate their territory, and pull out from their new colonies. The Romans were forced to surrender, passing under the humiliating "yoke" of one spear resting on two others, where they had to bow, one by one. Following this, Rome determined the treaty was invalid because it hadn't been made by the consuls, so the war resumed. Rome defiantly established colonies in Samnite areas, which did not go well for the colonists – the Samnites killed most of them.

In 312 BC, the Etruscans took advantage of Rome's preoccupation with Samnium and mobilized their forces against cities allied with Rome. In one battle, Rome prevailed, and the

Etruscans fled into the dark and fearful Ciminian Forest, which Romans dreaded entering. The consul's brother, Marcus Fabius, spoke Etruscan and volunteered to enter the forest posing as an Etruscan shepherd. He came to the town of Camerinum in Umbria, where the locals provided him with soldiers and supplies to fight the Etruscans. Together they crossed the forest and decimated the Cimian Mountain region.

The enraged Etruscans mustered their largest army in history, marching against the forces of Quintus Fabius (Marcus' brother). Quintus launched a surprise attack on the Etruscans at dawn, routing the Etruscans. Three Etruscan cities – Perusia, Cortona, and Arretium – agreed to a 30-year truce with Rome. Despite great losses, the Romans won a decisive victory against the Etruscans in the ferocious, drawn-out Battle of Lake Vadimo, thwarting the Etruscan strength. The entire Etruscan army sued for peace, agreeing to a one-year truce and offering a tribute of two tunics and one year's pay to every Roman soldier.

Now Rome gave its full focus to the Samnites. In 305 BC, both consuls marched on Samnium. Together, in a series of savage battles, their armies brilliantly vanquished the Samnites, who negotiated for peace. At the end of this war, Rome took over the regions of the Hernici and Aequi people, most of whom had allied with Samnium, and parts of Volsci and Sabine territory. But peace only lasted several years.

The Third Samnite War raged from 298 to 290 BC. The Etruscans were momentarily distracted by an invasion of the Gauls, but they bribed them to leave so they could assault Rome. As rumors floated that both the Samnites and Etruscans were raising colossal armies, Rome allied with the tribes surrounding Samnium. The Samnites allied with the Etruscans and hired the Gauls as mercenaries, but they were no match for Rome. With 15,000 troops and 12,000 allies, Rome marched on Etruria and routed their army, killing 8000 soldiers.

Meanwhile, the Samnites were raiding Roman colonies in Campania. In the Battle of Sentinum in 295 BC, Rome took on the combined forces of Samnites, Etruscans, Umbrians, and Gauls. In this deadly confrontation, Rome lost 8700 men but killed 20,000 of the coalition enemies. In the next few years, the Samnites rallied new forces but were defeated in daring attacks by the two Roman consuls, sealing the doom of the Samnites. Rome then turned to the Sabines, crushing them and annexing their territory. Rome conquered or allied with the remaining Latin tribes. The Roman war machine was now fixated on conquering the Mediterranean.

Chapter 6: Expansion to the South

Everyone enjoys victories, big or small, but a *pyrrhic victory* costs so much to win that the hard-fought triumph seems meaningless. That's what happened to Pyrrhus, King of Epirus, remembered as the ruler who defeated Rome and Carthage in multiple battles yet reportedly said, "If we win another such battle against the Romans, we will be completely lost."

The series of battles known as the Pyrrhic War (280-275 BC) involved Rome, the Greek states of Italy, Epirus, Egypt, Sicily, Carthage, and the tribes of central and southern Italy – mainly the Samnites and Etruscans.

The war started when Rome violated a naval agreement with the city of Tarentum. Rome controlled part of southern Italy, but Tarentum (in the heel of Italy's boot) was the most important city of the *Magna Graecia* (Greater Greece) colonies. Founded by the Spartans, Tarentum was a cultural and economic center – the primary commercial port for southern Italy. With about 300,000 people, it was among the most populated cities in the world at that time.

Rome's increasing power was worrying the Tarentines, especially after the Samnites – their former allies – were defeated. With the most powerful navy in Italy, Tarentum quickly formed an agreement with Rome prohibiting Roman ships from entering the Gulf of Taranto.

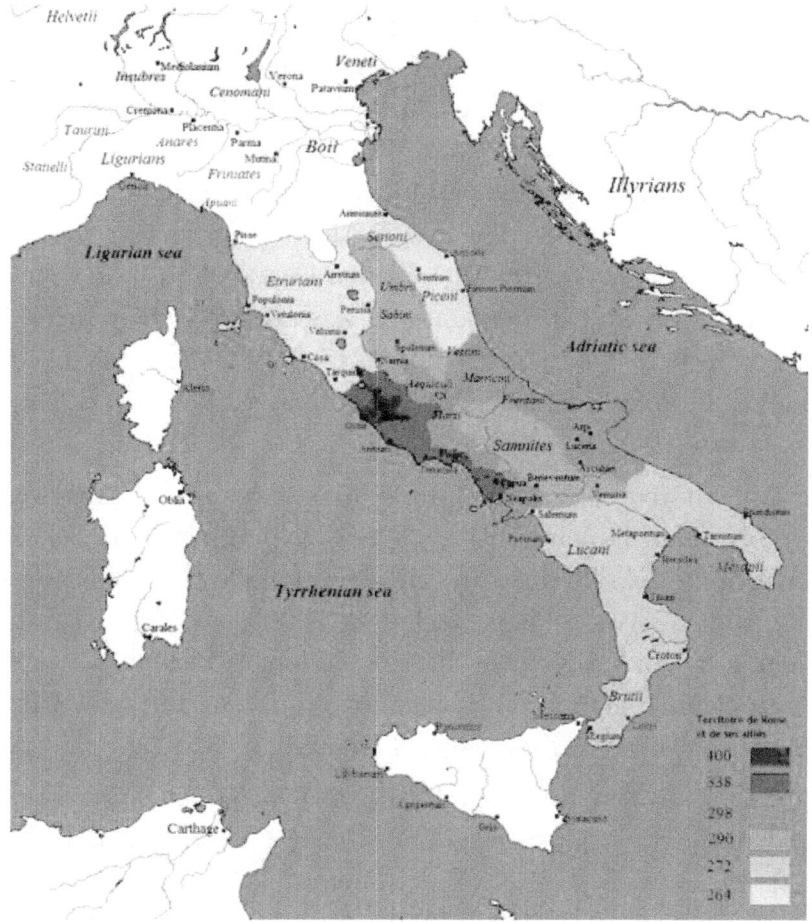

This map shows Rome's expansion of power over the Italian peninsula from 400 BC to shortly after the end of the Pyrrhic War.
https://en.wikipedia.org/wiki/Pyrrhic_War#/media/File:Conqu%C3%AAte_romaine_de_l'Italie_(400-264).png

In 282 BC, a Roman fleet was transporting troops to their garrison in Thurii, on the far side of the Gulf of Taranto from Tarentum; technically, Rome had broken the agreement even before a tempest blew ten ships toward Tarentum's shores. The infuriated Tarentines believed this was an intentional, aggressive act violating their pact, so they promptly sunk four Roman ships and captured another. The Tarentine navy then sailed across the gulf to Thurii, aided that city's democrats to overcome and exile the aristocrats, and forced the Roman garrison in Thurii to withdraw.

Rome sent their diplomats to work things out with Tarentum, but the hostile Tarentines broke off the peace talks and insulted Rome's ambassador. In retaliation, the Roman Senate declared war on the Tarentines, who called on an old ally who owed them a favor. Pyrrhus was the king of Epirus (now mostly Albania), just across the Ionian Sea from Italy's heel. Tarentum had aided King Pyrrhus in conquering the island of Corcyra (Corfu), so now it was his turn to help them. Pyrrhus agreed to help Tarentum, mainly because he was keenly interested in gaining a foothold in Italy – he had ambitions for his own empire like his cousin Alexander the Great.

After borrowing warriors, funding, horses, and elephants from his brother-in-law Ptolemy II, Pharoah of Egypt, Pyrrhus set sail across the Strait of Otranto toward Italy. He arrived in the Gulf of Taranto in 280 BC, with 25,000 soldiers, including 3000 elite soldiers and 20 war elephants (guided by their Indian mahouts). Pyrrhus sent envoys to Rome, letting them know he had arrived in Italy and was eager to help them mediate their dispute with Tarentum.

The Romans scoffed at this, mobilizing eight legions (about 80,000 soldiers) divided into four armies. They sent two armies to Vanusia and Etruria to engage the Samnites, Lucanians, and Etruscans, preventing them from assisting Pyrrhus. The third army stayed home to protect Rome, while the last army of 30,000 men, led by Publius Valerius Laevinus, marched toward Tarentum, plundering Lucania on the way.

This terracotta doll from Tarentum dates to the third century BC, about the time of the Pyrrhic War.
https://commons.wikimedia.org/wiki/File:Terracotta_doll_Louvre_Cp4654.jpg

Before charging into battle against the Romans, it became glaringly apparent to Pyrrhus that the Tarentines he had come to rescue were incapable of saving themselves. Plutarch said they were happy to let Pyrrhus go to war on their behalf while they stayed behind enjoying their baths and festivals and defending their city through valiant speeches. Pyrrhus sternly forbade frivolities as inappropriate during wartime: he closed their gymnasia and parks and outlawed drunkenness, festivals, and any revelry. He then called up all the able-bodied men for service in the military. Unaccustomed to being ordered about, many men left the city, considering it slavery not to live as they pleased.

When Pyrrhus received word that the Roman consul Laevinus was swiftly marching south with a huge army, he was irritated that his expected allied forces had not yet arrived. He decided not to wait on them because any delay would give time for the Romans to advance even further. He sent another envoy to the Romans, offering his services as an arbiter for the Greek states in Italy. Laevinus answered that they didn't need a mediator with the Greeks, nor did they fear him.

Pyrrhus had no choice but to march forward, setting up camp on the opposite side of the river Siris from the Romans. He rode up a bluff overlooking the river, where he could view the Roman camp. The Greeks used the word *bárbaros* (barbarian) to designate anyone who wasn't Greek – who lacked what they considered civilized ways. After observing the Romans' discipline and order, he remarked, "These barbarians aren't barbarous; we shall see what they amount to."

The first battle took place in Heraclea (in the arch of Italy's boot), about halfway between Thurii and Tarentum. With his Tarentine allies, Pyrrhus had 35,000 troops positioned on the left bank of the Siris river, which the Romans had to cross before the battle. He intended to begin with a charge of his 3000 men on horseback and 20 elephants.

As the Romans crossed the river at dawn, Pyrrhus' calvary successfully broke up their lines. Yet Pyrrhus met an army that was stronger and more disciplined than any he'd ever encountered. In the heat of the ferocious battle, Pyrrhus fearfully switched his armor with one of his lieutenants, so he wouldn't be recognized and targeted. The man wearing his armor became the focus of the Roman forces, who killed him. His men believed the dead man was their king and panicked, forcing Pyrrhus to take off his helmet, so they could recognize his face. The Greeks cheered and pressed on with the battle.

Pyrrhus sends out his secret weapon – war elephants! By Helene Guerber - Story of the Romans, Public Domain,
https://commons.wikimedia.org/w/index.php?curid=32722047

Finally, Pyrrhus released the mighty war elephants. The Romans had never encountered elephants in battle before; their foot soldiers staggered at the sight of the massive animals while their terrified horses stampeded away. Pyrrhus then sent his cavalry charging into the Roman forces, routing them and winning the victory for the Greeks. However, one of Pyrrhus's elephants was wounded, and the panicked animal charged, crushing a segment of Pyrrhus' own army.

The casualties were colossal for both sides, even though reports differed on how many died that day: ranging from 7000 to 15,000 Romans and 4000 to 13,000 Greeks. The Romans lost more men, but they still had three other armies ready to move into place. For Pyrrhus, replacing thousands of troops would be almost impossible. Fortunately for him, several Italic tribes – the Lucanians, Messapians, and Bruttians – joined forces with him, as did two Greek cities in southern Italy – Croton and Locri. Advancing north, he allied with the Samnites, Rome's former enemy.

Once again, Pyrrhus offered to make peace with Rome, and once again, Rome rejected the offer. Pyrrhus then tried to conquer Campania, but by that time, the Romans had reinforced their army in that region. Brazenly, he even attempted to take Rome but found its fortifications too strong. Meanwhile, the Romans had allied with the Etruscans and had sent word to the other consul Curuncanius. Pyrrhus realized three armies were rapidly closing in on him: Rome's garrisons, Consul Laevinus from the south, and Curuncanius from the north. He quickly withdrew from the area and wintered in Tarentum.

King Pyrrhus spent the winter rebuilding his forces, calling in troops from Macedonia and his allies on the Ionian Peninsula. In the spring of 279 BC, Pyrrhus set out once again to dominate Italy with a 40,000-man army confronting Rome's forces on the opposite banks of a river. Cassius Dio said the river's strong current made it difficult to ford. The Romans politely asked Pyrrhus if he preferred to cross over to their side for the battle. If so, they promised to back off and not interfere with his troops while they crossed. Pyrrhus said they could cross over to his side unmolested, as he had great faith that his elephants would win the day.

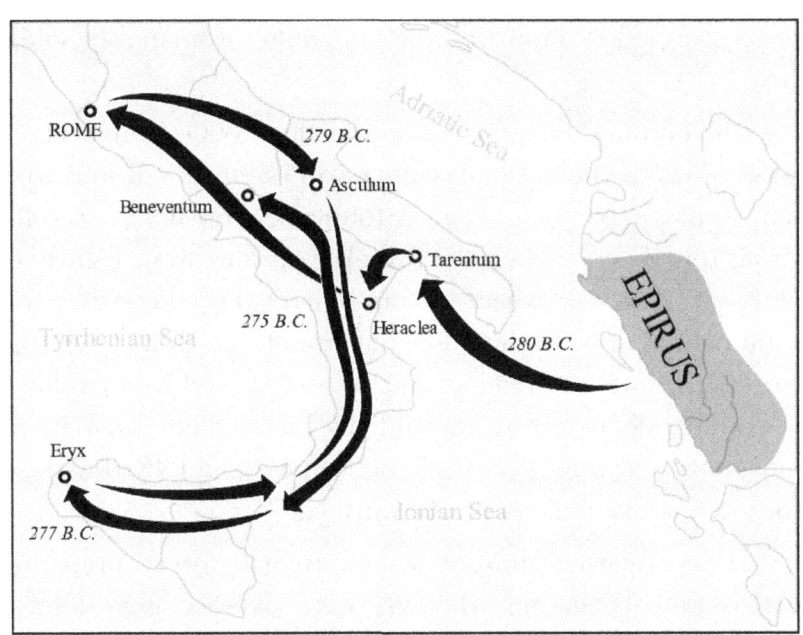

This map traces Pyrrhus' battles in the Pyrrhic War: Heraclea, Rome, Asculum, Sicily, and finally Maleventum (renamed Beneventum). https://commons.wikimedia.org/wiki/File:Pyrrhic_War_Italy_en.svg

For two days, the Romans and Greeks fought at a place called Asculum. This time, the Romans were prepared for the elephants. First, the Romans fought in forested terrain on uneven ground, which deterred the charging elephants and horses. Second, they had devised ingenious ox-drawn wagons, with tall iron beams that had spears attached, bristling in all directions; lined up, they blocked the elephants from advancing. Using small catapults, they could shoot fiery projectiles and other ammunition from their 300 anti-elephant wagons.

At the beginning of the battle, the Romans prevailed over the Greeks, slowly but firmly forcing them back. The fighting was fierce, and many were killed or wounded before nightfall interrupted the battle. In the morning, Pyrrhus brought the elephants out but had them enter the battlefield at each end, avoiding the wagons. The sight of the elephants terrified the Romans' horses even before they drew close, and once again, the Roman cavalry broke up as the frantic horses stampeded. However, the undaunted Roman foot soldiers held firm.

At the end of the battle, between 6000 to 8000 Romans lay dead or wounded on the field, but it seemed to Pyrrhus that Rome replenished their forces like a gushing fountain, remaining resolute and courageous. Even though the Greek casualties were lighter – around 3,500 – Pyrrhus was exhausted and unnerved by the savage battle. Just as the fighting was winding down at sunset, the Romans destroyed his camp as they were retreating, and he was pierced by a javelin. Most of his commanders were dead, and his Italian allies were hesitant and ambiguous – fearing the wrath of Rome should Pyrrhus lose. "One more victory like that, and we're finished!"

Pyrrhus requested more funds and military forces, preparing for his next assault. While the Romans were likewise regrouping, a man named Nicias, who had been among the allies supporting Pyrrhus, approached the Roman consul Fabricius, offering to assassinate King Pyrrhus. Fabricius found this an outrageous affront to Roman honor, taking pride in defeating the enemy through valor, military strength, and strategy. He sent envoys to Pyrrhus, alerting him of the plot.

Astonished, Pyrrhus released his Roman prisoners of war, sending them back to Rome with renewed offers of peace. For his treachery, Nicias was executed and flayed – straps formed from his skin were made into a chair. Rome replied to offers of peace by requesting Pyrrhus leave Italy. Rome also renewed their alliance with Carthage due to mutual concerns about Pyrrhus' potential involvement in Sicily, which might jeopardize Carthage's colonies there. This alliance was a blow to Pyrrhus, who had hoped to pit one nation against the other, distracting them from his schemes for Italy and Sicily.

Pyrrhus sailed to Sicily when Syracuse and other Greek cities on the island offered him rule over them in exchange for defending them from Carthage and ridding them of tyrants. The Macedonians also sent him an offer – the throne of their country – their king had just been captured and beheaded by the Gauls. Pyrrhus liked Sicily better: it was closer to Africa, and he had his sights set on eventually conquering Carthage.

Pyrrhus' abrupt departure from Italy aggravated the Tarentines, who had grown weary of his tyrannical rule over their city. They demanded he either continue fighting Rome or leave Italy for good. The Romans were amazed Pyrrhus suddenly interrupted the war but pleased for the opportunity to bring the Samnites back in line and gain control over the Lucanians and Bruttians who had thrown their lot in with Pyrrhus.

The Romans immediately set to work, conquering Croton and Lokrami – Greek cities that had allied with Pyrrhus. Tarentum and Regi alone remained as independent city-states. The Roman consuls Junius and Rufinus invaded Samnium, devastating the rural farms and taking over some deserted forts. While Junius remained in Samnium to continue wreaking havoc, Rufinus moved on to harass the Lucanians and Bruttians.

This ancient Greek theater in Syracuse, Sicily, built from 450 to 400 BC, was standing when Pyrrhus arrived.
https://commons.wikimedia.org/wiki/File:Ancient_Greek_theater,_450-400_BC,_Syracuse,_121541.jpg

Arriving in Sicily in 278 BC, Pyrrhus found Syracuse already under attack by Carthage. The Carthaginians realized that Pyrrhus' forces were modest in size and not especially strong, so they ruthlessly attacked his army repeatedly, attempting to drive him out of Sicily. Pyrrhus did capture two Sicilian cities – Panormus and Eryx – but eventually left the island after three years due to the Carthaginians' constant harassment. No sooner did he sail away than Panormus and Eryx overthrew his rule.

Pyrrhus arrived back in southern Italy, met by the irate Tarentines disgusted with him for pulling out in the middle of things and leaving the Samnites and Lucanians vulnerable to Rome. Most of the resentful Samnites had no future interest in allying with him against Rome. He had only 20,000 troops left, but he was determined to gain a foothold in Italy. He devised a strategy for his third and final attack.

Pyrrhus divided his army into two divisions – each would fight one army of the two Roman consuls: Cornelius Lentulus and Manius Curius. Pyrrhus led one division toward Maleventum (meaning *bad arrival* or *evil omen*), where Curius was stationed, marching through the night in hopes of a surprise attack before Lentulus could come to his aid. This tactic did not go well for Pyrrhus and his men.

Rather than taking the main road, Pyrrhus chose a longer route through the woods where they would be unseen and able to preserve the element of surprise. But after a few hours, their torches burnt out, and they got lost navigating through unfamiliar territory in the dark. They wandered off the paths used by people and mistakenly followed goat-paths that veered here and there, up steep crags of rock and down into deep ravines.

The troops got separated from each other, and by the time they finally staggered into Maleventum, it was an ominously bad arrival: they were weak and fatigued, overcome with thirst, and the elephants were jittery. To make matters worse, they stumbled out of the woods at dawn on the top of a hill, easily seen from miles around by Curius' troops assembled in the valley below, ruining all hopes of a surprise attack.

Within moments, Curius led a charge from their camp against Pyrrhus and his army, even capturing some elephants. The battle moved down toward the level ground of the plain, where Curius routed some of Pyrrhus' exhausted troops. Then an elephant charge forced the Romans to retreat to their camp, but the camp guards on the ramparts threw their javelins at the elephants, who turned around and charged off. The Romans had finally learned how to deal with war elephants by spearing their sides, a tactic they later used against Carthage. The out-of-control elephants charged back through Pyrrhus' ranks, crushing men and throwing the troops into pandemonium. The battle was disastrous for Pyrrhus. He so desperately needed a victory, but instead of even a pyrrhic victory, he suffered a humiliating loss to the Romans at Maleventum.

Then the Samnites demanded his aid. They had stuck their necks out for him, and now the Romans were making their lives miserable. When Pyrrhus arrived to assist the Samnites in the battle against the Romans, an adolescent elephant was wounded. Shaking off his Indian mahout (driver), he charged off trumpeting for his mother. Hearing him, the agitated mother elephant stirred up the other elephants, and soon everything was in confusion – another catastrophe. The Romans scored an extraordinary victory, capturing eight elephants, killing many soldiers, and occupying the Samnite's entrenchments.

Pyrrhus escaped to Tarentum with only a few horsemen and quickly sailed to Epirus, leaving behind a small detachment in Tarentum. His victories in Italy and Sicily were fruitless; he returned home with nothing to show for it. The Tarentines who had invited him much hoped he would stay away, as their situation was much worse than before he came to their aid. As a parting gift, Pyrrhus left the Tarentines the chair made from Nicias' skin.

Pyrrhus never returned to Italy, although he vowed he would. Three years later, while engaged in battle in Argos in southern Greece, an old lady on a rooftop threw a tile down at him, which hit him in the neck and knocked him from his horse. He lay paralyzed in the street until a Macedonian soldier cut off his head. When word of this traveled back to Italy, the Tarentines surrendered to Rome, continuing as a self-ruled city, but with Roman laws and a Roman garrison. The Greek city-states in Italy quickly followed.

Dogged perseverance had won the day for Rome. The Romans celebrated their victory over Pyrrhus by renaming the city of Maleventum (*bad arrival* or *evil omen*) to Beneventum (*welcome* or *good omen*). Soon, the Appian Way would connect the town to Rome. By 272 BC, the Latins, Etruscans, Samnites, and other Italic tribes came under complete submission, making Rome the established ruler of Italy, except for the Gauls to the far north.

Rome was now poised to go forward and conquer the civilizations surrounding the western Mediterranean Sea. Their only plausible contender was Carthage.

Chapter 7: The Punic Wars

In an enthralling struggle for supremacy, Rome and Carthage clashed in three epic wars spanning eight decades from 264 to 146 BC. The legendary feats of the Punic Wars included the Romans building 120 ships in 60 days, Hannibal crossing the Alps with his war elephants, and Scipio ingeniously deflecting an elephant charge back toward the Carthaginians, crushing their ranks. Both Rome and Carthage suffered horrific casualties, and the outcome affected the Western world for centuries to come.

Why were they called *Punic* Wars? *Punicus* is Latin for Phoenician – the people of Tyre who fled with Queen Dido to North Africa, where they built the new city of Carthage. When a tempest blew Aeneas's ships to her shores, a passionate romance ignited – until Aeneas abandoned Dido to sail to Italy. Just before Dido committed suicide, she prophesied unending wars between their descendants, and now those wars were happening.

It all started with Messana (Messina) in Sicily, just across the Strait of Messina from the toe of Italy's boot. The city had given refuge to the Mamertines – Italian mercenaries – who returned the kindness by attacking and killing the entire population, sparing only the younger women to be their wives. These desperados transformed the peaceful Messana into the hub of their pirate raids on land and sea.

After the Mamertine pirates ravaged Sicily's coast for 20 years, an exasperated Hiero II, king of Syracuse - 100 miles down the coast from Messana - resolved to rid Sicily of the marauders. Marching north, he successfully dispatched most of the Mamertines forces, then closed in on Messana. As it happened, a fleet from Carthage was harboring in Messana, and the Mamertines called on them for assistance. Unwilling to get involved with Carthage, Hiero withdrew.

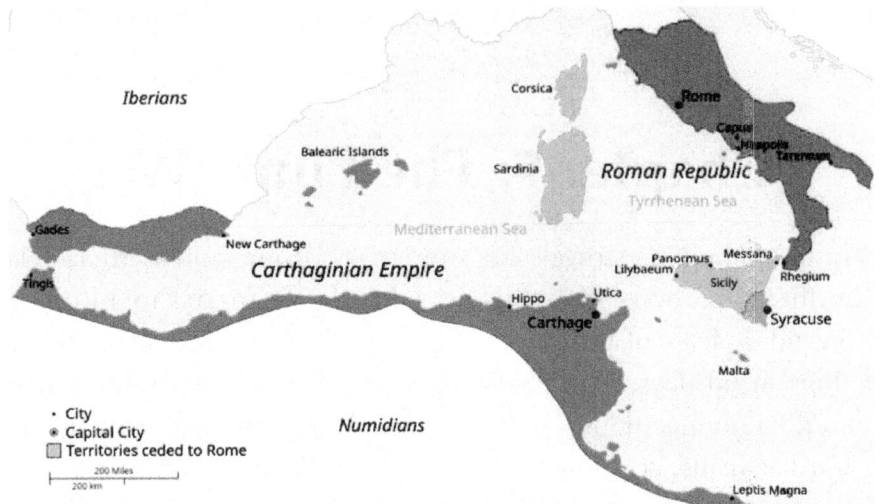

This map depicts Rome and Carthage's territory just before the First Punic War. https://commons.wikimedia.org/wiki/File:First_Punic_War_237_BC.png

The Mamertines expected the Carthaginians to leave, but instead, they established a garrison in Messana. The Mamertines weren't too happy with that state of affairs - it infringed on their pirating escapades. Four years later, Hiero attacked again; this time, the Mamertines appealed to Rome for protection. Rome was wary of the pirates but didn't want Carthage to expand its power in Messana, only six miles across the Strait of Messina from the toe of Italy's boot. Rome agreed to ally with the Mamertines, who then convinced the Carthaginian garrison to leave.

Rome deployed 16,000 men to Sicily - the first time their military had ever left the Italian peninsula. Alarmed, Syracuse approached Carthage for protection. Hanno, commander of the Carthaginian forces, first crucified the garrison commander who left Messana without orders. Next, the allied Syracusan and Carthaginian armies marched to Messana, where the Romans brutally defeated them.

Rome then attacked Syracuse. Hieron surrendered and allied with Rome, allowing him to remain in power. In 262 BC, Carthage sent new forces to Acragas (Agrigento) in southeastern Sicily. Both Roman consuls leading four legions savagely attacked Acragas and sacked the city, selling the population into slavery. This eye-opener influenced Segesta, in northeast Sicily, to revolt against Carthage and ally with Rome, swaying other cities to likewise defect from Carthage.

After several engagements with the Carthaginian navy – the greatest in the world at that time – Rome realized it needed a substantial naval force to take on Carthage's war machine. At manic speed, Rome astonishingly built a fleet of 100 heavy warships in only two months, using a shipwrecked Carthaginian quinquereme as a guide. The oar-powered, 50-meter-long quinqueremes could carry 420 sailors and soldiers, providing power, speed, and reasonable maneuverability in marine battles. They also built 20 smaller triremes propelled by oars and sails.

As novice sailors, Rome could not compete with the experienced Carthaginian marine tactics, so they had to devise an ingenious way to bring their superior combat skills into play. They developed an 11-meter-long *corvus* – a gangplank that could hook onto the enemy's ship – allowing the Romans to board and engage in the hand-to-hand combat in which they excelled. The ships also carried catapults for flinging missiles (often burning) that pummeled the enemy ships.

This Roman mosaic from Tunisia shows a trireme vessel during the Roman Empire. https://commons.wikimedia.org/wiki/File:Romtrireme.jpg

The brilliant corvus boarding tactic ushered in immediate victory over Carthage's 130 ships in the 260 BC Battle of Mylae (Milazzo) and again in the 258 BC Battle of Sulci, where the Carthaginians crucified the losing commander. Bolstered by these extraordinary successes, the Romans sailed from Italy toward Africa to attack Carthage itself, having increased their fleet to 330 ships carrying 140,000 men.

The Carthaginians mustered 350 ships, intercepting the Romans off the coast of Sicily in the unforgettable Battle of Cape Ecnomus – the largest naval battle in history, with 680 ships and 300,000 men in the two navies. After a long day of confounding conflict, the Romans won a decisive victory over Carthage, sinking 30 of their ships and capturing 64, while losing 24 Roman ships. About 10,000 Romans were killed, compared to three to four times as many Carthaginians.

Having scored a stunning naval victory, the Romans confidently sailed on to Africa, winning a land battle only 10 miles south of Carthage, where the rough terrain impeded their enemies' elephants. Unfortunately for the Romans, Carthaginians counterattacked, led by the Spartan general Xanthippus, with 100 elephants and 4000 soldiers, surrounding and wiping out 12,000 Romans and capturing 500. The

2000 Romans who escaped the massacre were picked up by the Roman fleet that had just returned from Italy, but another disaster loomed ahead. When they were out to sea, a violent storm sunk all but 80 of their 400 ships and drowned up to 100,000 men – the greatest loss of life in a single shipwreck incident in history.

Returning to Sicily, the indomitable Romans rallied, capturing Panormus (Palermo) in 254 BC, enslaving everyone except any citizens who could pay a 200-drachmas fee. Meanwhile, Carthage overcame and razed Acragas. Rome suffered another crushing loss when 150 more ships were sunk in a storm as they were returning from a raid in North Africa. Two Carthaginian attacks on Sicily in 251 and 250 BC failed – in the second, the Romans even captured their elephants, shipping them back to Rome to entertain the citizens.

But Carthage won a sea battle the following year, capturing 93 of Rome's 120 ships. The Romans blamed their consul Claudius Pulcher for bringing bad luck – he had thrown his sacred chickens overboard when they failed to give him a good omen and was put on trial for impiety when he returned to Rome. Then another disastrous storm sunk 800 Roman supply ships. By now, both sides were running out of supplies, ships, and men. The Egyptian Pharoah Ptolemy II declined Carthage's request to help with 2000 talents.

Hamilcar (Hannibal's father) was promoted as Carthage's remarkable new fleet commander. He brutally raided Italy's coast, then headed to Sicily in 244 BC to harass the Roman forces, earning the nickname *Barca* (lightning) for his swift guerrilla tactics that enabled him to capture Eryx, making it his base. Within two years, however, Rome had rebuilt their fleet to 200 ships, which they sensationally used to defeat the Carthaginian fleet, sinking 50 ships, capturing 70, and taking 10,000 prisoners of war. After two decades of war, a humiliated Carthage was forced to sue for peace in 241 BC – withdrawing completely from Sicily and paying Rome 3200 talents of silver. Thus, Sicily became Rome's first offshore province.

This win affected the large island of Sardinia, east of Italy, which had been settled by the sea-faring Phoenicians of Lebanon about the same time they were founding Carthage. Later, Carthage had taken control of these colonies and built new ones. When the First Punic War ended, these colonies revolted, allowing Rome to occupy the entire island without resistance.

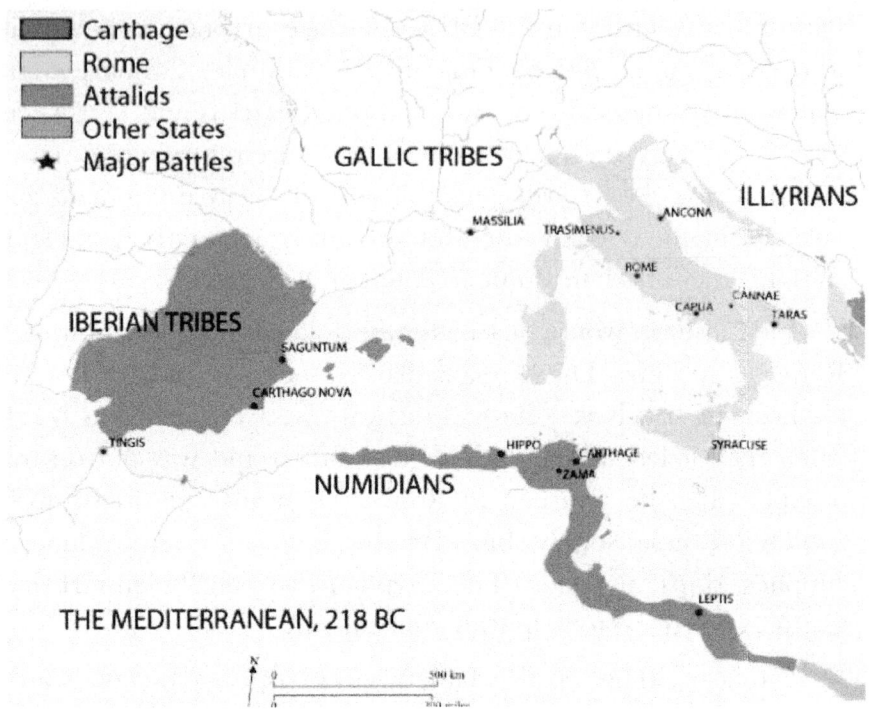

This map depicts Rome and Carthage's territory immediately before the Second Punic War. By Megistias - Moore, R. L. (1981). The Hamlyn Historical Atlas London: Hamlyn. ISBN 0-600-30361-6 p. 22., Public Domain, https://commons.wikimedia.org/w/index.php?curid=93770825

The Second Punic War began in Spain, where Carthage had been establishing colonies for several hundred years. The champion Hamilcar Barka victoriously extended Carthage's control to about half of the Iberian Peninsula, and his son Hannibal became Iberia's supreme commander in 221 BC. Following Rome's advice, the city of Saguntum on Spain's eastern coast resisted Carthage's control. Hannibal viciously retaliated in 219 BC by laying siege to Saguntum while Rome was distracted with an Illyrian revolt. Despite a serious javelin wound, Hannibal overcame Saguntum in eight months, killing every adult in the city.

Infuriated, Rome declared war. The Second Punic War – or the Hannibalic War – was a struggle between Carthage's formidable commander Hannibal and his nemesis – Rome's great general Scipio – who received the agnomen (honorable nickname) *Africanus* for his stunning North African military triumphs.

As Hannibal astutely anticipated, Rome sent 60 warships under Scipio's command to Spain – but by the time they arrived, Hannibal was executing his unbelievable surprise move far north of Spain. With 90,000 foot-soldiers, 12,000 cavalrymen, and 37 elephants, he marched up Spain's coast, fighting off local tribes, crossed the 11,000-foot-high Pyrenees into Gaul (France), and advanced toward the Alps.

Hannibal approached the Rhone River, knowing a tribe of Gauls was waiting to attack him on the other side. He diverted his lieutenant Hanno to cross the Rhone 25 miles upstream. Hanno then marched downstream, sneaking up behind the Gauls whose full attention was on Hannibal's men, boats, and especially the elephants – creatures the mountain people had never seen. The Gauls were riveted by the sight, ready to attack Hannibal as he crossed with his fleet of boats and rafts. Suddenly, Hanno's men launched a surprise rear attack, routing the Gauls so Hannibal's army could cross the river unmolested.

Now it was time to conquer the 13,000-foot-high Isère region of the Alps before the winter snows began. Depending on which route he took – and scholars are still arguing about that – the pass through the Alps would have been from 6500 to 9500 feet high. As the men, horses, and elephants labored up the steep slopes, fierce mountain tribes dropped boulders on them.

This is a potential site of the landslide on the Col de la Traversette pass, which reaches 3,000 meters above sea level.
https://commons.wikimedia.org/wiki/File:ColleTraversette2007.jpg

    Hannibal's descent down the Alps on Italy's side was free of human attack, but steeper and treacherous, with deep snow and a narrow, icy path along the edge of the mountains – one misstep would send man or animal hurtling to the rocks a mile below. At one point, a landslide blocked the path. Hannibal attempted a detour, but the heavy snow was impassable. Finally, they cleared the rocks from the mountainside to make a level path and got the men, horses, and pack mules down to the tree line beyond the snow. It took another three days to get the starved elephants down.

    Hannibal unexpectedly descended into Italy with the remnant of his army – 20,000 foot-soldiers, 6000 soldiers, and an unknown number of elephants. The Gauls of northern Italy, eager for another opportunity to take on Rome, joined Hannibal and the Carthaginians. Hannibal took swift advantage of Rome's lack of preparedness, overcoming the Romans in two disastrous battles in northern Italy in December 218 and in a third battle in June 217 at Lake Trasimene in central Italy – in that horrific battle, 15,000 Romans were killed and 10,000 captured.

The unstoppable Hannibal fought a spectacular campaign in August 216 against a much larger Roman army of 80,000 soldiers versus 50,000 Carthaginians in Cannae – in the heel of Italy's boot; 50,000 Romans were slaughtered compared to 5700 casualties (mostly Gauls). This influenced most of southern Italy's city-states to defect to Carthage, while the Latins and other tribes of central Italy stayed loyal to Rome.

Rome realized Hannibal's innovative strategies in battle made him indomitable, so their new strategy was to wear him down by using their navy to cut off access to new supplies and manpower. Meanwhile, in 209 BC, General Scipio Africanus scored a staggering win in Spain, capturing Carthage's treasury and supply base.

Elected as consul in 205 BC, the enterprising Scipio turned his attention to Africa. With 440 ships and 30,000 soldiers, he sailed to Tunisia, while Carthage mustered a force of 30,000 foot-soldiers and 3000 cavalrymen led by General Gisgo. Attacking in the dead of night with two divisions of Romans surging in from opposite sides, Scipio devastated the Carthaginians forces. Carthage rallied with reinforcements of African Numidians (a Berber tribe) who were outflanked and overwhelmed by Scipio's outstanding calvary.

Predicting that Rome would win the conflict, the shrewd Numidian King Masinissa defected to Rome, putting Carthage in grave danger from their former allies. Hannibal hurried to Carthage from Italy to defend his homeland, facing off against Scipio in the decisive final Battle of Zama in 202 BC.

Both the Romans and Carthaginians had to fend off the charging war elephants at the Battle of Zama
https://commons.wikimedia.org/wiki/File:Schlacht_bei_Zama_Gem%C3%A4lde_H_P_M otte.jpg

Although outnumbered, Hannibal's troops fought fiercely for their city, but Scipio deftly channeled Carthage's 80 war elephants through his ranks with minimal harm, then herded them back in a charge that laid havoc to Hannibal's men. While the Carthaginians were distracted with corralling the elephants, the Roman and Numidian horsemen circled round to the rear of Hannibal's forces, sandwiching them between Rome's foot-soldiers at the fore.

Rome won the day; 20,000 Carthaginians perished in the bloodbath, compared to 5000 Roman fatalities. Carthage conceded defeat; the terms of surrender included dismantling its navy, agreeing not to war against anyone without authorization from Rome, and paying a 50-year annual tribute to Rome of 200 talents of gold in war reparations.

Hannibal slipped away to exile in Ephesus, and Carthage paid its war debt for 50 years, maintaining friendly terms with Rome – even allying with Rome in several foreign military campaigns. But they chafed against Rome, forbidding them to war against the Numidians – who had been steadily capturing the territory surrounding Carthage under their King Masinissa. After half their territory had been taken, they sent 31,000 men in 150 BC to unsuccessfully defend the city of Oroscopa; most of these men were slaughtered by the Numidians.

Roman felt this act of aggression without permission – against Rome's ally – breached the treaty, even when Carthage explained their side of the story. Cato, one of Rome's censors, had been part of a senatorial embassy that visited Carthage in 152 BC to negotiate peace with the city and King Masinissa. The Second Punic War veteran was shocked at the wealth Carthage had accumulated – since they were no longer spending all their manpower and funding on conquering other lands, Carthage had been growing its economy.

Cato considered the city a great threat to Rome. "Carthago delendam est!" he cried out. "Carthage must be destroyed!" Repeatedly, Cato had been denouncing Carthage, ending all his speeches – even on unrelated topics – with "Carthago delendam est!" – "Carthage must be destroyed!"

At first, the Senate resisted Cato's demands for Carthage's destruction. The powerful Senator Corculum, the son-in-law of Scipio Africanus, argued that fear of Carthage preserved Roman unity. He ended all his speeches with, "Carthago sevanda est!" "Carthage must be saved!" However, once Carthage attacked King Masinissa and the Numidians, the senatorial debate swung to Cato's side. Carthage had gone to war without permission, and worse yet, against an ally of Rome.

The Senate sent an embassy to Carthage with their ultimatum: dismantle their army, surrender their arms, leave Carthage, and resettle inland. Carthage rejected Rome's terms, and the Third Punic War began with Rome sailing to North Africa with 80,000 foot-soldiers and 4000 cavalrymen, laying siege to the city of 200,000 for three years.

Initially, Carthage held up well with 21 miles of massive walls surrounding and protecting their city along with the sea on two sides and moats surrounding the rest. The Roman forces failed to block all the supplies coming into the city. Carthage counterattacked with fireships – older ships set on fire and quickly abandoned by the crew, which sailed into the Roman fleet, setting it on fire. The surrounding cities weren't capitulating as quickly as Rome had hoped. Despite sustained attacks, the Carthaginian city of Hippacra would not surrender to Rome. The Numidians' new king Bithyas sent 800 cavalrymen to assist Carthage. Then, to the Carthaginians' glee, the Romans were hit by an epidemic in the 148 BC summer's heat.

This bronze statue found on the Quirinal in Rome is believed to be Scipio Aemilianus.
https://commons.wikimedia.org/wiki/File:Bronze_statue_of_a_Hellenistic_prince,_1st_half_of_2nd_century_BC,_found_on_the_Quirinal_in_Rome,_Palazzo_Massimo_alle_Terme,_Rome_(31479801364).jpg

This wasn't turning out to be the quick and easy war Rome was expecting. What could they do to turn things around? Step one was to elect Scipio Africanus' capable grandson Scipio Aemilianus as the new consul and commander of the Roman forces. He was about five years too young to meet the minimum age requirement of 41 for consul, but Rome disregarded the age limit, certain he would carry the day as his grandfather had in the past war.

Scipio Aemilianus set to work immediately, building an improved siege wall and a mole (breakwater) on the south side, blocking access to Carthage's harbors. The Carthaginians secretly built 50 new warships inside their walls, then opened a second harbor entrance and sailed them out against the Roman fleet. The Romans prevailed against the new fleet and successfully kept supply ships from entering the new passageway. Scipio then relentlessly attacked the walls, concentrating on the harbor. At night, the Carthaginians would silently swim across the harbor and set fire to the catapults and other siegeworks.

Finally, after three years, Rome broke through Carthage's walls in 146 BC, and soldiers poured into the city, fighting street by street and house by house against the citizens, who fiercely defended their city and homes. After a week of brutal hand-to-hand combat, Carthage was overcome. The 50,000 remaining citizens were sold into slavery, and Carthage was plundered and burned to the ground. Polybius wrote that Scipio wept as he watched the city burn, remembering the Fall of Troy and perhaps wondering if the same fate eventually awaited Rome.

The Fall of Carthage brought an end to that great city and its Phoenician civilization. Apart from a short-lived Roman colony soon after the war, the ruins were abandoned for a century until it was rebuilt as a Roman city by Julius Caesar and Caesar Augustus. With no more competition from Carthage, Rome now controlled the western Mediterranean, developing into a powerhouse of trade and military expansion, dominating much of the known world.

Chapter 8: Rome versus Greece

While embroiled with Hannibal in the Second Punic War, Rome was simultaneously engaged in intense wars with the Macedonian Kingdom, the Seleucid Empire, and the Achaean League in Corinth. Rome's struggles with these Greek empires, driven by complicated politics, continued until the same year that Carthage fell at the end of the Third Punic War.

When the Ptolemaic Empire of Egypt tottered, the Macedonian and Seleucid Empires surged forward to grasp power, prompting several Greek city-states to seek Rome's protection. Rome's involvement with these eastern empires wasn't so much a long-term plan of expansion but short-term goals in an unpredictable situation that affected Rome's alliances and provinces. Rome fought on Greece's mainland for the first time in the Macedonian wars.

The First Macedonian War (214-205 BC) began while Hannibal was wreaking havoc in Italy – pursuing a scorched-earth strategy of destroying anything that could sustain Rome's military machine: food stores, water sources, weapon manufacturing, and transportation venues. King Philip V of Macedonia entered into a treaty with Hannibal because Rome's increasing interference with Illyria and Epirus was disturbing Philip's empire-building schemes.

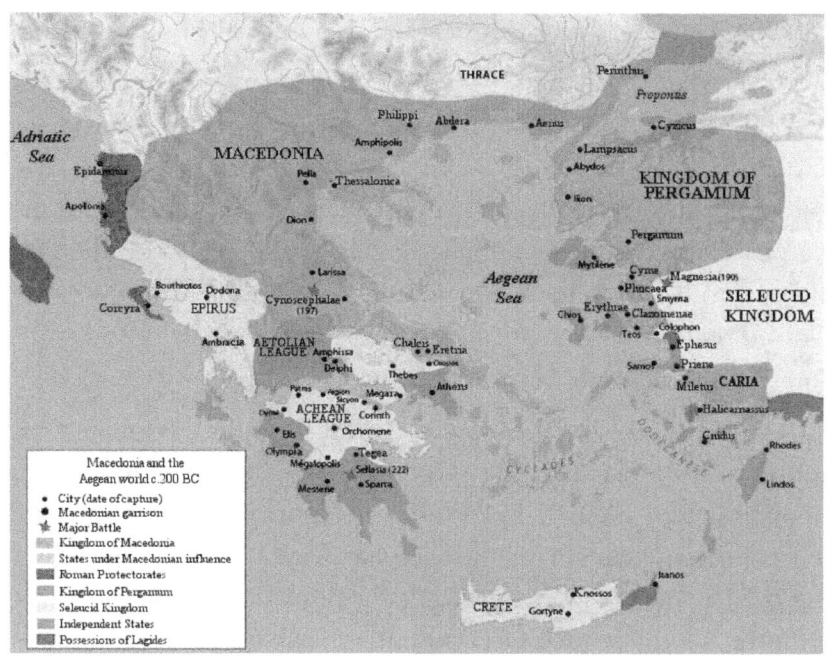

This map depicts Macedonia and the Aegean world just before the First Macedonian War. Public Domain,
https://commons.wikimedia.org/w/index.php?curid=3731726

Philip capitalized on Rome's crisis with Hannibal by targeting Rome's allies on the Adriatic coast. His treaty with Carthage stipulated mutual support – each would be the enemy of the other's enemies – the chief enemy being Rome. Philip's envoys had snuck into Italy to negotiate the treaty with Hannibal; on their way out, they were captured by the Romans, who seized the treaty document. The Romans weren't especially concerned about the alliance but determined to keep a short leash on Philip.

In 214 BC, Philip initiated a siege on Apollonia – a city in Illyria on the Adriatic Sea; Rome sent reinforcements to Apollonia, forcing Philip to retreat. The following year, Philip captured two strategic fortresses in Illyria. Rome needed an ally in the area, and the Aetolian League – a Greek tribal confederation on the Corinthian Gulf already hostile to Philip – seemed the best candidate. King Attalus of Pergamum (eastern Turkey) agreed to assist the League. Rome supplied 25 warships, while the Aetolians provided soldiers.

While Philip was off campaigning on his northern borders, the Aetolian League invaded Acarnania – Philip's ally in Greece's mainland. The Acarnanians hurried their women and children off to Epirus, swearing they would defeat the invaders or die trying. They prevailed over their menacing invaders until Rome's navy got involved, capturing the cities of Nasus, Oeniadae, and Zacynthus – which Rome handed over to the League.

In 211 BC, the joint forces of Rome and the Aetolian League captured Anticyra on the Gulf of Corinth. Rome sold the population into slavery, but Philip recaptured the territory. Philip then campaigned to drive the Aetolian League from Thessaly (on Greece's western coast), allying with Bithynia (northern Turkey). Sparta (in southernmost Greece) entered the war, siding with Rome and the Aetolian League, creating chaos for Philip.

Philip's formidable Macedonian-Bithynian forces successfully defeated the Aetolian-Spartan coalition in Greece's southern Peloponnese peninsula in 209 BC – convincing the Aetolian League to enter peace negotiations, which broke down when Rome's commander Sulpicius sailed in with a Roman fleet. However, Philip brilliantly defeated the Romans, taking Sicyon in the Peloponnese before he had to hurry home to defend against an invasion from Dardania on Macedonia's northern border.

In 208 BC, the fleets of Rome and Attalus patrolled the Aegean Sea, but Philip's forces nearly captured Attalus after slipping through the Thermopylae Pass – the "gates of fire" – a narrow passage with hot sulfur springs between Mount Kallidromo and the Gulf of Malia. Then Bithynia invaded Pergamum, compelling Attalus to withdraw completely from the war to fight off the invaders. Rome's fleet harbored on the island of Aegina, leaving the Corinthian Gulf undefended against Philip's campaigns; he captured several cities, then headed to the Peloponnese to fight the Spartans.

This didrachm of Philip V of Macedon is on display at the British Museum. https://commons.wikimedia.org/wiki/File:Philip_V_of_Macedon_BM.jpg

Rome withdrew from the Aegean Sea, concentrating on protecting Illyria's coast on the Adriatic, their primary objective all along. With Attalus pulling out and Rome retreating to the Adriatic, the Aetolians and the Spartans were the only challengers to Philip and his Greek allies. Captain Philopoemen of Megalopolis in the Peloponnese defeated the Spartans, killing their commander Machanidas. Now the Aetolians were wide open for Philip's ferocious attacks – he drove them out of Thessaly and the Ionian Islands and sacked Thermum – their federation capital.

Pummeled by Philip and with no support from Rome, the Aetolian League sued for peace, stirring Rome to send an army of 10,000 foot-soldiers and 1000 cavalrymen to Illyria, but the League refused to join with Rome against Philip. Realizing that Carthage was losing the Second Punic War, Philip determined it was in his best interest to end his war before that happened – while he was ahead.

The Macedonians, Aetolians, and Romans formed the Peace of Phoenice Treaty in 205, ending the First Macedonian War. Philip had expanded his power to Greece's mainland and inland Illyria, while Rome was satisfied the Illyrian coast was no longer threatened. The treaty held for five years, until Rome finally conquered Hannibal, ending the Second Punic War.

A secret pact instigated the Second Macedonian War (200-197 BC). King Ptolemy IV of Egypt died in 204 BC, succeeded by his six-year-old son Ptolemy V. This led to chaos over who would be regent while the boy was growing up. Philip V of Macedonia plotted with Antiochus the Great of the Seleucid Empire to conquer Egypt's empire in its vulnerable state. If successful, Philip would get Cyrene and the Aegean Sea territories, and Antiochus would claim Egypt and Cyprus.

Before taking on Egypt, Philip wanted to subdue the Greek colonies bordering Macedonia in Thrace and near the Dardanelles Strait. His masterly conquest of Chios in the Aegean Sea disturbed nearby Rhodes and Pergamon – they had been eying Chios for themselves. Meanwhile, Antiochus was plowing through Coele-Syria, taking Damascus, Sidon, and Samaria. Alarmed, the Aetolian League solicited Rome's help against Philip and Antiochus, but Rome initially ignored their pleas.

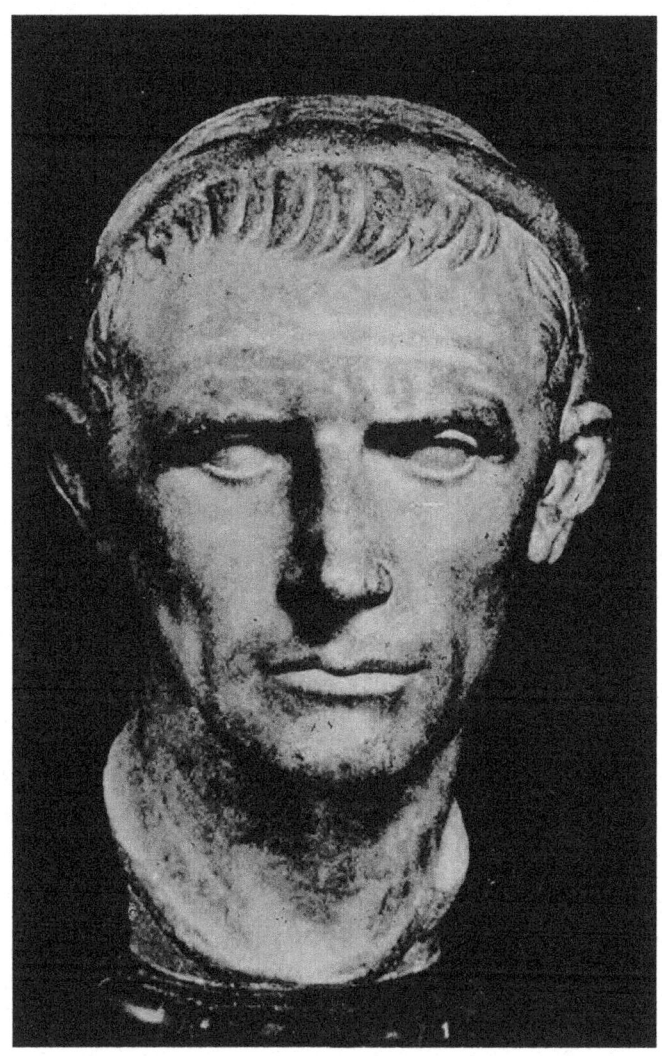

Antiochus III (The Great), the ruler of the Seleucid Empire, plotted with Philip V to divide the Egyptian empire.
https://commons.wikimedia.org/wiki/File:Greece_from_the_Coming_of_the_Hellenes_to_AD._14,_page_287,_Antiochus_III.jpg

In 201 BC, Philip laid siege to the island of Samos, Egypt's marine base, and conquered the island of Miletus – both in the Aegean Sea. Meanwhile, Antiochus defeated the Anatolians in the Battle of Panium at the Jordan River's headwaters, ending the Egyptian Ptolemaic rule in Judea. The Jews opened the gates of

Jerusalem to Antiochus – preferring Seleucid rule over Egyptian. Little did they know that his son, Antiochus *Epiphanes* (*God manifest*) – but called by his haters Antiochus *Epimames* (*the madman*) – would place an idol to Zeus and sacrifice a pig in Jerusalem's holy temple – defiling it and leading to the Maccabean Revolt.

By now, Rome had wrapped up their final, victorious war against Carthage. They still didn't think Philip and Antiochus threatened their interests, but they sent Commander Laevinus to investigate if there was cause for a "just war." Eventually, Rome sent Philip an ultimatum – he could keep Macedonia and Thrace, but he had to withdraw from Greece and stop aggressions in other places – especially Egypt.

Philip ignored Rome's ultimatum, which he received while laying siege to Abydos – the crossing point between Europe and Asia – in the Dardanelles. He warned Abydos the walls would be stormed in three days; anyone who wanted to surrender or commit suicide needed to do so by then. The citizens killed their women and children, threw their gold and jewels into the sea, then fought Philip's army until the city fell.

At this point, the Roman Senate, finally swayed by their new Consul Sulpicius, voted for war against Philip. Sulpicius mustered his troops – many who had just returned from fighting Carthage in Africa – and sailed across the Adriatic. Philip and Sulpicius faced off in 200 BC in the Dassaretae territory, but after a couple of skirmishes, Philip received word that the Dardanians were invading Macedonia, so he and his men slipped away at night to defend his borders.

The Romans were surprised to wake up the next morning to find Philip's troops gone. Sulpicius chased after Philip, ravaging his land on the way. Philip sent half of his army to the north to fight Dardania and led the other half south to meet Sulpicius. But by this time, Sulpicius had turned back and was back on his fleet launching attacks on Macedonian military bases.

Meanwhile, in Rome, elections were held for the next two consuls. Consul Villius was sent to Corcyra to replace Sulpicius. When he arrived, Villius encountered 2000 disgruntled veterans of the Third Punic War, resentful that they'd been given no break between wars. Villius spent most of his one-year term sorting out the Roman military, then two new consuls were voted in.

The newly-elected Titus Quinctius Flamininus, only 31 years old (much younger than the age requirement of 41 for consuls), won the lottery for Macedonia. He speedily drove Philip out of most of Greece, and then confronted Philip in the Battle of Aous in Albania. The Macedonian army was in an impregnable position behind a pass, but a shepherd showed the Romans a secret path that led to the rear of their position, allowing them to launch a surprise attack with 2000 Macedonian casualties.

Flamininus' term was ending, but he was performing so well that Rome appointed him as proconsul, granting him authority to continue fighting Philip. In the 197 BC Battle of Cynoscephalae, fought against Philip in Thessaly, Flamininus had 20 of his own war elephants! At dawn, no one could see anything due to heavy fog that covered the hills and valley where the two armies met. But the elephants routed the Macedonian phalanx, and at least 8000 Macedonians were killed. Philip sued for peace, forced to abandon the Greek territories he had acquired and to stay within his borders.

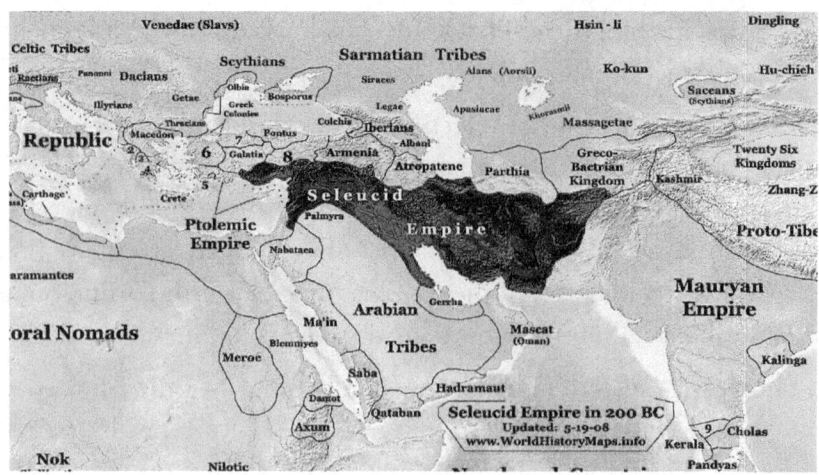

This map depicts the Seleucid Empire in 200 BC, just before the war with Rome. By Thomas Lessman - Own work, CC BY-SA 3.0, https://commons.wikimedia.org/w/index.php?curid=4079843

With Philip subdued, Rome turned its attention to his co-conspirator, Antiochus the Great of the Seleucid Empire. Rome had no problem with Antiochus retaining his previous empire, along with Egypt, but they wanted him out of Thrace. Antiochus felt Thrace belonged to him – for a brief window of time, it had belonged to his ancestors.

The Aetolian League in Greece, former allies of Rome, were now hostile to Rome and allied with Antiochus. They invited Sparta and Macedonia to join them. King Nabis of Sparta, resentful that Rome had taken his coastal cities, happily joined forces with the Aetolians. King Philip V didn't dare incur Rome's wrath again; instead, he assisted Rome against Antiochus.

In 192 BC, Nabis of Sparta won back several of his coastal towns. However, General Philopoemen of the Achaean League (Greek city-states in the southern Peloponnese peninsula) overpowered him, chasing him back to Sparta. Nabis appealed to the Aetolian League. In a heinous act of betrayal, they sent 1000 foot soldiers and 300 cavalrymen to Sparta, seemingly to aid the king, but assassinated him instead.

Meanwhile, Antiochus marshaled his forces and sailed to Greece with 10,000 troops, 500 cavalrymen, and six elephants, landing in Demetrius and taking on the Achaean League. Rome immediately sent two legions and ran Antiochus out of Greece within six months.

The war now shifted to Asia Minor, where Rome, allied with Pergamum and Rhodes, sent their imposing forces commanded by Lucius Scipio and his brother Scipio Africanus (hero of the Second Punic War). Hannibal had gambled on fighting for Antiochus; now, he commanded the striking new Seleucid fleet he had constructed in Phoenicia. However, the Rhodian fleet intercepted and defeated Hannibal, leaving only Antiochus' main fleet in Ephesus.

In the ensuing marine battle, Antiochus lost half his fleet – sunk or captured by the fleets of Rome and Rhodes. The final clash between Antiochus and Rome climaxed in Magnesia, Thessaly, where half of the Seleucid army was destroyed. Antiochus agreed in 188 BC to hand over his cities in Asia Minor to Rome and pay a war debt of 15,000 talents to Rome and 4000 talents to Pergamum. Despite this defeat, Antiochus was still the powerful king of the Seleucid Empire, spanning from Egypt east to Persia (Iran) and north to the Taurus Mountains of modern-day Turkey.

In 171 BC, Rome entangled once again in the Third Macedonian War. Philip had died, leaving his ruthless and enterprising son Perseus as King of Macedonia. Perseus was never meant to be king – he was the son of a concubine, and his brother Demetrius, son of Philip's wife, was the legal heir. But Rome had taken Demetrius hostage while only a small child – part of the peace deal ending the Second Macedonian War.

Perseus expected to ascend to the throne, but five years later, Rome returned Demetrius to his father. When Demetrius grew up, Philip sent him as his ambassador to Rome's Senate. The Romans were fond of Demetrius, and he won great esteem from the Senate. Insanely jealous of his half-brother's soaring diplomatic accomplishments, Perseus knew Demetrius would likely be the next king. How could he get rid of him?

Perseus attempted to ruin Demetrius through deplorable intrigues; when that failed, he falsely accused Demetrius of trying to kill him. When no one believed him, he manipulated Philip's General Didas to accuse Demetrius of treason with Rome against Macedonia – showing "evidence" of a forged letter from Flamininus. Philip fell for this ruse, putting Demetrius into Didas' custody. Perseus then deceived Didas into believing Philip had ordered Demetrius' death – which he conducted secretly.

Now Demetrius was dead, Philip was dead, and Perseus was king – and he hated Rome. King Perseus strategically allied with the Seleucid Empire by marrying King Seleucus' daughter Laodice. He arranged a marriage for his sister Apame IV to their cousin, Prusias II of Bithynia –Macedonia's ally in the First Macedonian War.

Unexpectantly, King Abrupolis of Thrace attacked Macedonia, devastating the country and capturing its gold mines. Perseus fought back and drove Abrupolis out of Macedonia. Although Perseus was rightfully defending his own country, Rome was offended because he trounced their ally.

Perseus enlarged his military and allied with King Cotys IV, ruler of Thrace's largest state. He circulated propaganda he could reform Greece, restoring its legendary wealth and power. His generosity to the Greek states and cities influenced their support; they visualized him as one of their own, a revolutionary who wanted freedom from Rome.

Meanwhile, King Eumenes II of Pergamum (Macedonia's neighbor to the east) was in Rome, triggering hostilities against Perseus – astutely pointing out his influence, marriage alliances, and how he was stockpiling weapons for war. Perseus determined to get his revenge by assassinating Eumenes. His plot to kill Eumenes failed, but Rome got wind of it, declaring Perseus public enemy number one and voting for war against Macedonia.

In 171 BC, Perseus triumphantly seized all the primary cities in northern Thessaly. Meanwhile, the Roman commander Publius Licinius led his troops in an intense march from Epirus through treacherous mountains to Thessaly's capital city of Larissa. Eumenes of Pergamon joined him, bringing 4000 foot-soldiers and 1000 cavalrymen. In the Battle of Callinicus, Perseus withdrew from the Roman forces but declared a Macedonian victory because Rome lost 2000 men compared to 400 Macedonian casualties.

A little later, most of the Romans had left their camp to harvest the ripening grain in the region. Catching them off-guard, Perseus raided their camp, capturing supplies and 600 men. Publius Licinius rushed to the area with his men and elephants, attacking Perseus and trapping his heavy infantry in a narrow passage. In this deadly battle, 8000 Macedonians died, and 4000 Romans perished.

In the decisive 168 BC Battle of Pydna on Macedonia's coast, Perseus suffered a crushing defeat at the hands of the talented new Roman commander Aemilius Paullus. The cowardly Perseus abandoned the battle early on, leaving the Romans to kill 20,000 of his men and capture 11,000. Pydna's plunder was so valuable that the exhilarated Roman citizens got a massive tax break. The Romans then hunted Perseus down to the island of Samothrace. The islanders handed him over, and Perseus was hauled to Rome in chains.

A ROMAN TRIUMPH.

Following great military victories, Rome would host a "triumph" – a grand procession through the streets displaying the captives and plunder, with the victors wearing crowns of laurel.
https://upload.wikimedia.org/wikipedia/commons/4/45/A_Roman_Triumph.png

The triumph (celebration of a military victory) in Rome was the most magnificent the Romans had ever seen – lasting three days, displaying Perseus led in chains and trophies of the war, including Perseus' chariot accompanied by exuberant soldiers wearing laurels. Rome's spectacular victory spelled the end of the Antigonid Dynasty in Macedonia; Rome divided the kingdom into four republics under Rome's control.

In 146 BC, the Achaean League declared war against Rome – a suicidal act, considering Rome's recent triumphs over Carthage and Macedonia. Although former allies, the Achaean Greeks held a bitter grudge against Rome for taking many of their citizens as hostages in the Third Macedonian War. The Achaeans also grappled with Rome over their desire to expand, while Rome wanted them to shrink back to their original states.

Led by their generals Critolaos and Diaeus, the Achaeans desperately fought two Roman armies led by Praetor Metellus and Consul Mummius. Caught off-guard by Mummius' astounding maneuvers, the main Achaean force led by Critolaos fled to

Scarpheia, where the ones who didn't commit suicide were killed or captured by the Romans. Critolaos disappeared, never to be seen again. The Achaean League panicked, and many towns surrendered immediately.

Part of the League, especially Corinth, rallied around Diaeus as the massive Roman forces led by Mummius advanced on Corinth. Within a few hours, the Achaean troops who didn't escape were captured or killed. Diaeus fled to Arcadia, where he committed suicide. Most of the Corinthians slipped out of the city before the Romans – suspicious of an ambush – entered three days later. The Romans massacred all the remaining men, enslaved the women and children, then sacked the city, plundering her precious works of art to carry home to Rome; many valuable pieces were damaged or destroyed in the chaos.

The Achaean League dissolved, and the weakened foundations of Greece crumbled before Rome. For the next century, the city-states and kingdoms of Greece and the rest of the eastern Mediterranean constantly shifted alliances, no longer the unparalleled world powers they once had been. However, in the realms of religion, philosophy, literature, and art, Greece exerted a paramount influence over Rome for centuries to come.

Chapter 9: The Civil Wars

In his tirade on civil war in the *City of God*, Augustine mockingly asked why Rome erected a Temple of Concord following Gaius Gracchus' murder. "Why didn't they build a Temple of Discord instead?" Ancient Rome engaged in epic wars of conquest during its Republic era, but the vicious bloodbaths that strikingly transformed Rome were those fought against itself.

Social unrest in Rome swirled around land ownership. The *ager publicus* (public land) Rome acquired through conquering new territories was usually distributed to aristocrats, who also confiscated lands the peasants were working – forming large plantations farmed by slaves. This left the hapless peasants with no means of support. They couldn't join the military because they weren't landholders, yet the military desperately needed more men.

The Gracchi brothers, Tiberius and Gaius, struggled for social reform – they advocated for limiting the public lands an individual could hold to about 325 acres and redistributing the rest of the land to the displaced peasants and war veterans whose land was often stolen while they were fighting abroad. Tiberius was elected Tribune of the Plebs in 133 BC, but the aristocratic senators, fearful of losing their lands, stirred up a brutal mob who clubbed Tiberius and 300 of his supporters to death.

Ten years later, Gaius was elected Tribune, and once again, the insidious senators raised a mob to kill him – but he committed suicide first. The brothers' deaths were not in vain – their cause would be championed by forward-thinking politicians in the coming decades.

Gaius Marius, Roman war hero and statesman, was elected as consul seven times.
https://commons.wikimedia.org/wiki/File:Glyptothek,_M%C3%BAnich,_Alemania,_2013-02-02,_DD_19.JPG

Gaius Marius – a rising star in Roman politics – began his brilliant career as a plebeian military tribune, married to Julia, Julius Caesar's aunt. After Jugurtha violently usurped the throne of Rome's ally Numidia (now Algeria in Africa), Rome engaged the pretender in war. Marius enabled a sensational victory after Jugurtha cut the Romans off from the river – their water supply – and split them into small groups in the desert. Marius formed a unified column of 2000 soldiers who broke through the Numidians, causing them to withdraw.

Elected as Consul in 107 BC, Marius needed more soldiers for his army but found Rome's military reserves depleted because only landholders could serve. Marius convinced the Senate to exempt his army from the land requirements. With his new troops, Marius marched across the African desert, relentlessly pressing Jugurtha southwest into Mauritania. Marius's shrewd cavalry commander – Lucius Cornelius Sulla – cunningly convinced King Bocchus of Mauritania to turn Jugurtha over to Rome, which Bocchus did, annexing Numidia to Mauritania.

While Marius was in Africa, aggressive tribes from Denmark and Germany – the Cimbri, Teutones, and Ambrones – arrived in the Rhone valley, pillaging settlements at Italy's northern border. Elected as consul again in 104 BC, Marius returned from Africa in triumph, with Jugurtha in chains, then headed to the Italian Alps with Sulla to drive out the savage Germanic tribes.

The legendary Battle of Aquae Sextiae began accidentally when the Romans, fetching water, encountered the Ambrones bathing in the same stream. In a spontaneous battle, the Romans killed 30,000 Ambrones. A combined force of Teutones and Ambrones counterattacked the following day, and 37,000 well-trained Romans butchered at least 100,000 of the Germanic tribes. Marius then bombarded the Cimbri, winning a decisive victory in the Battle of Vercellae, slaughtering 120,000 Cimbri and enslaving the rest. With a great triumph, Rome proclaimed Marius as the "third founder of Rome."

Rome's Senate passed the unpopular *Licinia Mucia* decree in 95 BC, expelling all non-citizens from Rome. In 91 BC, the Plebeian Tribune and reformer Drusus zealously advocated for greater distribution of state lands, enlarging the Senate, and granting citizenship for all of Italy. Drusus was assassinated, leading to a revolt of the Italian states – particularly the Marsi and Samnites – in the Social War of 91-87 BC.

Marius was called up to quell the rebel states. With Sulla, he killed 6000 rebels and captured 7000 before illness forced him to withdraw. To end the war, Rome decreed that all free people in Italy's mainland who were loyal to Rome would become citizens, receiving the right to vote. This led to the Romanization of Italy, as the Italic tribes integrated into Roman culture, abandoning their languages for Latin.

Tetradrachm of King Mithridates VI of Pontus, who fought with Rome in three wars.
https://commons.wikimedia.org/wiki/File:Tetradrachm_of_Mithridates_VI_CM_SNG_BM_1038.jpg

While concluding the Social War, Rome's attention fixated on the determined King Mithridates VI of Pontus on the Black Sea. Mithridates had invaded Cappadocia – Rome's ally – on his southern border. The First Mithridatic War (89-85 BC) began when Rome sent troops to Cappadocia. King Mithridates ordered the horrific extermination of all Romans living in Asia Minor – even women and children – killing 80,000 Romans as his forces savagely conquered one Roman city after another all the way to Greece.

In 87 BC, Consul Lucius Sulla – Marius's chief lieutenant in two wars but now his bitter rival – landed in Greece, recovered Athens and southern Greece for Rome, then headed north to crush Mithridates' army in the shattering Battle of Chaeronea (86 BC), despite being outnumbered. Continuing to score land and sea victories, Sulla forced Mithridates to accept a humiliating peace treaty in 85 BC, abandoning all lands except Pontus.

Leaving his general Murena to maintain stability, Sulla hurried back to Rome to confront the civil war roaring on in his absence. In 83 BC, the Second Mithridatic War was initiated when Murena heard rumors that Mithridates was building up his army again. Not waiting for Sulla's permission, Murena impetuously launched a preemptive strike on Mithridates, who swiftly defeated him at the River Halys. Sulla angrily ordered Murena to withdraw, ending the war indecisively.

The politician-generals Marius and Sulla both had razor-sharp fighting instincts that empowered joint success on the battlefield. But by 88 BC, they were engaged in a savage rivalry that plunged Rome into brutal civil war when Marius circumvented Sulla – consul for that year – by stealing his command of the Roman forces against King Mithridates.

Enraged, Sulla marched on Rome with his forces – an unprecedented and forbidden move for a Roman general and consul. Marius desperately rounded up gladiators to counter Sulla, but they were no match for his ferocity. Marius narrowly escaped to

Africa, while Sulla consolidated his command of the forces heading to Greece, then set sail to pummel Mithridates.

In his absence, Rome erupted into a vicious civil war between the Plebeian *Populares* and the Patrician *Optimates*. Marius slipped back from Africa, clandestinely organized an army, and marched into Rome in 87 BC, taking control of the city. He murdered his political enemies, displaying their heads on spikes, and manipulated his election as consul for the seventh time in 86 BC. But within two weeks, he suddenly died – apparently of pleurisy.

In 83 BC, Sulla wrapped up the war with Mithridates and crossed the Adriatic to Italy. Rome dispatched two armies to stop him; Sulla swept aside the first army, and the second army defected to his side. Marching on Rome once again, Sulla fought and won a fierce battle just outside Rome's walls and was quickly appointed dictator by the Senate.

Sulla exercised total control over Rome for two years before voluntarily resigning one year before he died in 78 BC. Blood flowed as he executed everyone considered an enemy of the state – 80 the first day, 220 the next day – the purge continued for months. One target was the teenage Julius Caesar, who fled Rome.

As a Patrician Optimate, Sulla was contemptuous of the Gracchian reforms championed by the Plebeian Populares. He empowered the aristocracy, strengthening the Senate over the Plebeian Council. He prevented the Plebeian tribunes from initiating new laws and vetoing Senate acts. Sullied increased the number of senators from 300 to 600, and extended Rome's sacred boundary – the *Pomerium* – which had not been moved since the monarchy period.

Rome and the rest of Italy had slaves – many slaves – captured from conquered cities and provinces. One intrepid slave from Thrace, named Spartacus, was sold to a gladiator school. Spartacus and 78 other gladiators succeeded in a daring escape one night in 73 BC, armed with cleavers and spits stolen from the kitchen. At least one gladiatrix escaped (yes, Rome had a few female fighters) – Spartacus' wife, also from Thrace. She was a prophetess of the god Dionysus and would occasionally be possessed by him. Once, Spartacus awakened, horrified, with a snake coiled on his face; his wife prophesied it was a sign of the formidable power that would drive him to greatness but kill him in the end.

The gladiators hiked to Mount Vesuvius, which was in a quiet stage at that time, joined by other slaves, raiding the area for weapons and provisions. The praetor Clodius besieged the mountain with 3000 soldiers, thinking the slaves were trapped on Vesuvius, where they'd run out of food. But the enterprising slaves wove vines into strong rope ladders, long enough to reach from the cliffs to the valley below, and they all escaped. The vagabonds roamed through Italy, ambushing Roman units, appropriating supplies, and freeing the rural slaves – as their numbers mushroomed to about 10,000.

The exasperated Senate sent both consuls and thousands of troops after the escaped slaves. The escapees divided into two groups – one remained in southern Italy with Crixus – spelling their doom – while the rest joined Spartacus in a long hike north toward the Alps. Spartacus planned to cross out of Italy, and everyone could then escape back to their respective countries, but some of the escaped slaves were growing over-confident and wanted to stay in Italy as desperados or revolutionaries.

One Roman army captured and killed Crixus and most of his rebel force, then marched north, entrapping Spartacus' group between the other Roman army. What the Romans didn't anticipate were horses! Spartacus had been building a cavalry; he unexpectantly charged the Romans, routing them and stealing their baggage. Spartacus reached the base of the Alps but inexplicably didn't cross over – perhaps the steep peaks proved too daunting.

The audacious new plan was to head south, cross over to Sicily, rekindle the slave revolt of 50 years earlier, and take over the island. Reaching the straits between Italy and Sicily, they hired pirates to sail them across but made the blunder of paying them in advance. The pirates sailed off with their money but without them, shattering their hopes of escaping Italy.

Spartacus and his band encamped at Rhegium, at the toe of Italy's boot, with the Roman commander Crassus closing in, whose strategy was to entrap the slaves and starve them out. Crassus built a 37-mile-long ditch across the peninsula from sea to sea – 15 feet wide and 15 feet deep – which filled with seawater. Then he built a wall along the canal. But the resourceful slaves waited until one stormy winter night, built a dam across the canal with dirt and trees, and crossed over.

General Crassus panicked, thinking they'd head to Rome and sack it. He was relieved to discover the volatile slaves had quarreled and divided into smaller groups. Crassus chased Spartacus' band up a mountain, but the slaves suddenly whirled around to fight, catching the Romans off-guard and routing them. The reckless slaves now felt invincible. Spartacus couldn't stop them from challenging the Romans.

Realizing a full-on battle was inevitable due to his men's overconfidence, Spartacus dismounted and killed his horse – saying if he won, he'd steal a horse from the Romans, but if he were killed, he wouldn't need the horse. In the blood-soaked struggle, Spartacus and most of his fellow slaves perished on the battlefield, but 6000 were captured and crucified, their crosses lining the Apian Way from Rome to Capua.

Crassus' triumph over Spartacus got him elected as consul in 70 BC, along with Gnaeus Pompeius (Pompey) Magnus. Pompey had just scored an impressive victory in Spain against Marius' supporter Sertorius, who was conducting guerilla warfare against the Roman Hispania provinces. On his overland route to Spain, Pompey forged a new route through the Alps, leaving a bloody swathe of carnage among the fierce mountain tribes. He spent five years in Spain in heated battles until the rebel forces lost morale and conspired to murder Sertorius.

Pompey's next challenge was to cripple the Cilician pirates raiding Italy's coast – a long-term and growing threat. In 67 BC, Pompey commanded 500 ships to vanquish the havoc wreaked by the pirates in the eastern Mediterranean. In only three months, he overcame the pirates based in Cilicia (southern Turkey), then rounded up marauding pirates in the Mediterranean, rehabilitating them by resettling them as farmers.

Immediately, Pompey turned his attention to King Mithridates in Pontus, who was stirring up trouble again. Rome gave Pompey supreme command in the east, and in 66 BC, he sailed to Asia Minor, marching through Bithynia to Pontus with eight experienced legions. Outnumbered, Mithridates put up a fierce resistance near the town of Dastira, but Pompey crushed his forces – later renaming the town *Nicopolis* (Victory City). Mithridates abandoned his kingdom, escaping to Armenia with the remnants of his army, where his son-in-law King Tigranes refused him refuge. Mithridates fled to Crimea, fruitlessly plotting his come-back until he committed suicide in 62 BC.

Once he'd defeated Mithridates, Pompey consolidated and reorganized the frontier kingdoms into Roman provinces. Amenia became a client state of Rome, with King Tigranes keeping his crown. Pompey then turned to Syria – once the heart of Antiochus III's grand Seleucid empire. After Antiochus' death, Syria had destabilized. The 163 BC Maccabean Revolt triggered by his son Antiochus IV's defilement of the Jerusalem temple made Judea semi-independent. The Parthians conquered Iran and took Babylon in 139 BC, reducing the Seleucid Empire to a small territory of Syria. Pompey conquered Syrian strongholds and cities until he reached Damascus, completing Syria's takeover and making it a Roman province.

He then turned to Judea, embroiled in a civil war between two royal brothers. Aristobulus II had usurped his brother Hyrcanus II's throne, and then, egged on by the wily Antipater – an Idumean – Hyrcanus had allied with the Arabian King Aretas to retake the throne. Pompey's General Scaurus came on the scene and kicked Aretas out of Judea. When Pompey arrived shortly after, he brought Judea under Roman control. Later, in 47 BC, Julius Caesar appointed Antipater as the first Roman Procurator. His son, Herod the Great, was notorious for ordering the massacre of all baby boys under two in Bethlehem following the birth of Jesus.

While Pompey was restoring order in Asia, the devious and deadly senator Lucius Sergius Catilina had his sights set on ruling Rome. During Sulla's bloodbath, he had decapitated his brother-in-law, then murdered his wife and son to marry the beautiful daughter of Consul Orestes. He bribed his way to acquittal at his trial. Incensed that the murder accusations prevented him from standing for consul election, he plotted to assassinate both consuls.

That conspiracy fizzled, but in 64 BC, Catiline ran for consul again, was defeated by Cicero and Hybrida, and defeated again the following year. Unable to rule legally, he conspired with disgruntled Patricians and veterans to overthrow the Roman Republic – planning to incite a slave revolt, burn Rome, then murder Cicero and the unsupportive Senators in the chaos. Cicero got wind of the plot and exposed Catiline, who fled Rome, but several other conspirators were arrested and, without trial, executed by strangling, despite Julius Caesar's forceful protest. Catiline and his men were later killed by the Roman army.

Rome's First Triumvirate was an alliance of Gnaeus Pompeius Magnus, Marcus Licinius Crassus, and Gaius Julius Caesar.
https://commons.wikimedia.org/wiki/File:The_First_Triumvirate_of_the_Roman_Republic_720X480.jpg

Rome's First Triumvirate formed as an alliance between its three most powerful men, all popular war heroes: Julius Caesar, Crassus, and Pompey. Pompey was aggravated when the senators balked at providing farmland for his war veterans and ratifying the treaties Pompey had made in the east. Caesar had just returned from a brilliant military campaign in Spain; supported by Pompey and Crassus (the richest man in Rome), he won the election as consul in 59 BC, then used his influence to secure Pompey's treaties and land for his men.

After serving as consul, the Senate posted Caesar to Roman Gaul as proconsul. He conquered Gallic tribes beyond Rome's province, expanding Rome's territories to all of today's France and Belgium, protecting Rome from Gallic invasions. He slaughtered two-thirds of the ferocious Helvetii warriors of the Swiss plateau. His 55 BC massacre of the Germanic Usipetes and Tencteri tribes, including women and children – prompted Cato to demand Caesar be turned over to the barbarians. In 55 BC and 54 BC, Caesar made daring expeditions to Britain, where he penetrated to what is now London.

Julia – Pompeii's wife and Caesar's daughter – died in childbirth, the first stage of failure for the Triumvirate. The following year, Crassus died on the battlefield. In 50 BC, the Senate ordered Caesar to return home – telling him to first dissolve his army. Caesar brazenly crossed the Rubicon River from Roman Gaul into Italy in January 49 BC – without disbanding his army – he came with one legion (about 5000 men), quoting Athens' playwright Menander: "The die is cast."

Pompey ordered the senators to evacuate to southern Italy. Caesar walked into Rome unhindered, helped himself to the treasury, then set out after Pompey. Before Caesar could catch up to him, Pompey sailed to Macedonia. Rather than chasing after Pompey, Caesar headed to Spain, where Pompey's army was stationed. "I'm going to fight an army without a leader, so I can later fight a leader without an army." Without much of a fight, Pompey's forces capitulated to Caesar.

Meanwhile, Pompey was busily assembling an army of his friends and allies throughout the East, commanding a fleet of 300 ships. Caesar had only a few ships – not even enough to get all his army to Greece. He left half of his army behind, waiting until Mark Antony could join him months later with four more legions – causing Pompey to withdraw quickly. But then Pompey's son sailed into the Adriatic with an Egyptian fleet and sank or captured virtually all Caesar's ships. Pompey won the Battle of Dyrrachium but failed to pursue Caesar's army, causing Caesar to remark, "The enemy would have won the war today if they had a commander who knew how to use a victory."

Pompey then risked a battle with Caesar on Thessaly's plains. Following their victory in Dyrrachium, Pompey's men foolishly assumed triumph was theirs. Despite being outnumbered, Caesar's seasoned military, following his innovative tactics, outmaneuvered Pompey's army, putting them to flight. Pompey fled by horseback to the coast. Caesar pardoned all who surrendered to him, including

Marcus Junius Brutus, who would one day be his undoing. Pompey sailed to Egypt, but instead of finding refuge, the Egyptians murdered him, sending his head to Caesar.

Julius Caesar and Cleopatra VII became lovers while Caesar was in Egypt. By Jean-Léon Gérôme - Public Domain, https://commons.wikimedia.org/w/index.php?curid=1399233

Caesar headed to Egypt to avenge the death of his former ally and rival Pompey, where he became entangled in a civil war between the 12-year-old Pharaoh Ptolemy XIII and his sister (and wife) Cleopatra VII. Dazzled by Cleopatra's exotic charms, Caesar became her lover, forcing Ptolemy out and restoring the throne to Cleopatra. The following year, Cleopatra gave birth to Caesarion – Caesar's only biological son. Caesarion became Pharaoh at age three, ruling with his mother until he was executed as a teen by Caesar's adopted son Octavius.

Caesar served as consul in 48 BC, and again from 46 to 44. He was dictator for several short-term periods and then appointed dictator for life in 44 BC – but his life was cut short that very year. As consul and dictator, Caesar implemented major reforms: alleviating debt and unemployment, revising the calendar, and initiating massive building projects in Rome, eager to match the grandeur of Alexandria. Caesar forgave his political enemies – extending *clementia* (mercy) – rather than reap revenge. But they had not forgiven him.

Fearing Caesar planned to crown himself king, at least 60 Senators had formed a conspiracy led by Marcus Junius Brutus, Gaius Cassius Longinus, and Decimus Junius Brutus. Desperate to retain the Republic form of government, even though many approved of Caesar's reforms, they plotted his murder. It was to take place in the Senate on March 15, 44 BC – the Ides of March. But when the senators assembled, Caesar didn't show up. Where was he?

Julius Caesar was assassinated by a Senate conspiracy, stabbed 23 times. https://commons.wikimedia.org/wiki/File:Death_of_Julius_Caesar_2.png

Early that morning, Caesar's wife Calpurnia woke up screaming from a nightmare of Caesar's body flowing with blood. She begged her husband to stay home. Caesar, remembering a recent prophecy that his life would end by the Ides of March, sent Mark Antony to dismiss the Senate. One conspirator – Decimus Brutus – came to Caesar's house, mocking him for listening to a woman, and Caesar accompanied him to the Senate. Within moments of walking in, the senators surrounded Caesar, stabbing him repeatedly – 23 times.

Caesar's murderers hoped his death would preserve the Roman Republic, but the opposite happened. The people of Rome could no longer trust their senators and became openly hostile toward them. Two days after Caesar's murder, Mark Antony – Caesar's right-hand man and consul for 44 BC – convinced the Senate to accept a compromise: amnesty for the conspirators in exchange for Caesar's laws remaining in effect.

Two days later, the reading of Caesar's will revealed he had named his grandnephew and adopted son Gaius Octavianus as his heir. At that time, 19-year-old Octavian was stationed with Caesar's army in Macedonia, waiting for Caesar to come to lead them against the Parthians. On March 20, Mark Antony gave the eulogy at Caesar's funeral, stirring the citizens into a riot as he held up Caesar's bloodstained toga.

Most conspirators fled the country, leaving Mark Antony as the primary leader for the remainder of the year. Marcus Lepidus, Caesar's Master of the Horse, was named *Pontifex Maximus* (high priest), and Antony and Lepidus arranged an engagement between Antony's daughter and Lepidus' son.

Gaius Octavianus returned to Rome in May, claiming his inheritance. Even though Caesar's will left his fortune to Octavian, Mark Antony refused to release the funds. Octavian borrowed heavily to honor Caesar's will that left money to every citizen of Rome. Friction between Mark Antony and Octavian escalated, with the Romans preferring Octavian over Antony. Cicero gave speeches depicting Antony as a threat to Rome. Two of Antony's legions defected to Octavian, but as a private citizen, he couldn't legally command them.

Antony's one-year term as consul was ending. Customarily, when consuls completed their term, Rome appointed them to govern a province. The Senate assigned Antony to Macedonia, but he wanted Cisalpine Gaul in northern Italy instead, which had been assigned to Decimus Brutus - Caesar's assassin. Antony marched north to take the province by force, while the fiery Cicero led the Senate to declare Antony an outlaw. They gave Octavian legal command over his forces and sent him with Rome's two new consuls to defeat Antony. Both consuls were killed in the battle, but Octavian prevailed, and Antony fled over the Alps into Transalpine Gaul (northern France), where his friend Lepidus was the new governor.

With Antony gone, the devious Senate felt the time was ripe to reassert their power - but they needed to get rid of Octavian, Caesar's heir, and the rest of Caesar's supporters. They put Caesar's assassin Decimus Brutus in charge of Rome's legions and Pompey's son Sextus over Rome's fleet. Octavian realized the only way he'd survive was to join forces with the man he'd just chased over the Alps. He initiated secret negotiations with Antony and Lepidus. Fortunately, Octavian's legions – who had been led by Caesar before – remained loyal to Octavian, refusing to be led by Caesar's assassin.

Octavian boldly marched on Rome with his legions in August 43, took the city, proclaimed himself consul, and put Caesar's assassins on trial, convicting them *in absentia*. In November, he traveled to northern Italy to meet with Antony and Lepidus. Together, they negotiated a three-man dictatorship – the Second Triumvirate – officially ending the Roman Republic.

They split up the available provinces among themselves: Octavian got Africa, Lepidus got Spain, and Antony took Gaul. They would have to fight their enemies for the rest of the Rome provinces: Sextus Pompey controlled the Mediterranean islands with his fleet, and Brutus and Cassius held the eastern Mediterranean provinces with the remainder of Rome's forces.

The Triumvirate first concentrated on avenging Caesar's death on the conspirators who had stayed in Rome or returned – executing one-third of the Senate, including Cicero, and confiscating their lands and fortunes to replenish Rome's treasury. Then they sailed to Macedonia to retake the Mediterranean from Brutus and Cassius, first breaking the blockade of Sextus' fleet.

In the first Battle of Philippi, Antony and Octavian attacked Brutus and Cassius from two directions. Antony scored a profound victory over Cassius' troops, and Cassius committed suicide. With Octavian ill and unable to lead, his troops lost to Brutus' forces, but 20 days later, Brutus lost the second Battle of Philippi and committed suicide. Now the triumvirs held control of all Rome's land forces and only had Sextus Pompey's fleet to conquer.

The Triumvirate had more provinces to divide among themselves. Antony got the lion's share, keeping Gaul and adding all the eastern provinces. Octavian and Lepidus traded – now Octavian had Spain and Lepidus ruled Africa. They technically ruled over Italy together, but Antony remained in the East, ruling the extensive Roman provinces from Ephesus.

In 41 BC, Antony asked Cleopatra for a meeting in Tarsus to iron out the alliance between Rome and Egypt. She had been living in Caesar's villa in Rome with their son Caesarion but had returned to Egypt after Caesar's murder. Cleopatra sailed up the river in a magnificent boat with silver oars, purple sails, and a golden prow – dressed as Aphrodite. The alliance was not only renewed, but Antony deliriously fell under Cleopatra's enchantment, living with her in Alexandria through the winter. Cleopatra gave birth to their twins – Alexander Helios and Cleopatra Selene – in 40 BC.

While Antony was frolicking with Cleopatra, Octavian was distributing land to Caesar's war veterans – until he ran out of land. Wanting to keep on the soldiers' good side, he confiscated land belonging to Roman citizens, even whole towns. Egged on by Fulvia – Antony's rich and powerful wife – the Senate opposed Octavian's land grants, which led to Octavian divorcing Fulvia's daughter Claudia (from Fulvia's first marriage). Octavian had married Claudia when she was only thirteen to seal the Second Triumvirate; two years later, he sent her back to her mother, saying the marriage had not been consummated.

The outraged Fulvia, the most powerful woman in Rome, allied with Mark Antony's younger brother Lucius Antonius – Rome's consul that year – in a war against Octavian. Some whispered her war was a ruse to draw her husband Antony away from Cleopatra and back to Rome. Octavian besieged Lucius's legions in Perugia – starving them out – while they waited desperately and futilely for Antony's return.

Finally, Lucius surrendered and was sent by Octavian on an appointment to Spain. Fulvia fled to Greece, meeting up with her annoyed husband Antony, who rebuked her for the war; she died of a sudden illness shortly after. Antony returned to Rome, smoothed things over with Octavian, and married Octavian's sister Octavia within weeks of Fulvia's death.

Sextus Pompeius still had control of the fleet and was blocking shipments of grain and supplies coming into Italy. In exchange for lifting the blockade, Octavian granted him control of Sicily, Sardinia, Corsica, and the Peloponnese. Octavian had married Scribonia, a relative of Pompeius, after divorcing Claudia. After two years, he divorced Scribonia on the very day she gave birth to his only biological child, Julia (he adopted four sons of his wives). That stirred up trouble with Pompeius again.

Octavian agreed with Antony to send 20,000 legionaries for Antony to fight Parthia in exchange for 120 ships to fight Pompeius. Antony kept his side of the deal, but Octavian only sent 10,000 legionaries. Fighting together, Octavian and Lepidus destroyed most of Pompeius' fleet. Lepidus then tried to claim Sicily, unsuccessfully, which got him kicked out of the Triumvirate.

Meanwhile, because Octavian had reneged on his end of the deal, Antony's shortage of manpower turned his Parthian expedition into a catastrophe. Cleopatra could replenish his army, so he resumed his affair with her, sending Octavia back to Rome and angering Octavian. Giving Cleopatra the title *Queen of Kings*, Antony awarded the province of Armenia to their son Alexander Helios. In 36 BC, they had another son – Ptolemy Philadelphus.

Acting on information from a defector from Antony, Octavian raided the Vestal Virgins' temple where Antony's secret will was hidden. It revealed Antony's plan to give away more of Rome's provinces to his sons and stipulated Antony was to be buried in Alexandria with his "Queen" Cleopatra. Antony also declared Caesarion to be Caesar's legitimate son and heir – a great threat to

Octavian who was Caesar's son by adoption. With this information, the Senate revoked Antony's powers and declared war on Cleopatra in 32 BC; however, a third of the Senate and both consuls defected to Antony

In 31 BC, Octavian faced off against Antony and Cleopatra in the naval Battle of Actium. Octavian's General Agrippa outmaneuvered Cleopatra's fleet, and the two lovers fled with 60 ships to Egypt, which Octavian successfully invaded a year later. Antony fell on his sword, dying in Cleopatra's arms. Realizing she would be paraded through Rome in chains, she committed suicide from a snakebite. Octavian honored her request to be buried next to Antony, but he killed 16-year-old Caesarion – her son from Caesar. After parading the children of Antony and Cleopatra in gold chains in the streets of Rome in his Triumph, Octavian gave Cleopatra's children from Antony to his sister Octavia (Antony's former wife) to raise.

The Republic of Rome, which had expanded exponentially and adapted to many changes in five centuries of existence, was crumbling. Rome would survive, but its semi-democratic government would die – the victim of incessant civil wars and internal strife. A new imperial political structure would now rise to lead the Roman Empire for the next four centuries.

PART THREE: THE PRINCIPATE (27 BC – AD 235)

Chapter 10: The Julio – Claudian Dynasty

If someone asked you to name a famous Roman emperor, perhaps you'd think of Julius Caesar and "Et Tu, Brute?" ("You too, Brutus?") Or maybe Nero leaps to mind, playing his lyre while Rome burned. In this chapter, we'll learn what led to Julius Caesar's assassination and Brutus' betrayal, and why Nero didn't mind that Rome burned.

Some of the best-known and notorious emperors piloted Rome through the next two centuries. Rome enjoyed its pinnacle of wealth, power, literature, and arts, but its Golden Age was marred by debauchery, cruelty, paranoia, and conspiracies. In 27 BC, the Roman Republic transitioned to the Roman Empire, led by the five emperors of the Julio-Claudian dynasty: Augustus (Octavian), Tiberius, Caligula, Claudius, and Nero.

Following the suicide of Antony and Cleopatra, Octavian returned to Rome, intending to gradually become the sole ruler without anyone realizing his aspirations. On the surface, he supported Rome's Republic and its senators. Elected as consul shortly after his return, his first objectives were to restore stability and, temporarily, the traditional legal and political system. He handed full power back to the Senate, giving up his command of Rome's armies and provinces.

Octavian was still running the show through delegated power from the Senate, his monumental wealth, and the relationships he had courted throughout the Roman world. He put his fortune to work buying the hearts of the people – for instance, privately funding Italy's road system. Because most of the empire's provinces were in chaos, the Senate asked him to resume his control over them for the next ten years, to which he agreed, pretending reluctance. Of course, commanding the provinces gave him control of most of the military.

This sculpture of Octavian (Caesar Augustus) was made shortly after he became Princeps.
https://commons.wikimedia.org/wiki/File:Augustus_Caesar.png

In January 27 BC, in the *First Settlement*, the Senate gave Octavian two new titles: *Augustus* (*illustrious one,* implying religious authority) and *Princeps Senatus / Princeps Civitatis (first in the*

Senate, first among the citizens). In the past, the *Princeps* title designated the leader of the Senate, but with Octavian, it acquired the meaning of first in the land – a pseudonym for emperor – which he refused to be called. Taking *Caesar* as his family name from Julius Caesar, his adopted father, he was now known as Caesar Augustus. He refused to wear the tokens of supreme power that Julius Caesar had worn – the purple toga and gold crown – but he continued as consul for several years, despite the position ordinarily being limited to one year.

In 23 BC, the Senate granted a *Second Settlement*, giving Augustus the power of tribune and censor – meaning he could call a meeting of the Senate, present business to the Senate, veto Senate actions, speak first at Senate meetings, supervise public morality, and hold a census. He was granted *sole imperium* – authority over all armed forces within the city of Rome, and *imperium proconsulare maius* – power over the governors of the provinces. Although he refused the title of emperor, he gradually acquired all the powers an emperor would hold.

Augustus used his powers productively. He restored law and order to Rome and the empire, enabling Rome to press forward. He reorganized the economic system, so the empire prospered financially, embarked on massive building projects of marble to beautify Rome, and established the Roman postal service, police and fire departments, and the Praetorian Guard.

He nearly doubled the size of the empire – conquering and consolidating northern Spain, Portugal, Switzerland, Bavaria, Austria, Slovenia, Albania, Croatia, Hungary, Serbia, and other points in western Asia and the Middle East. He expanded provinces in Africa to the south and east – forming an extensive trading network. He integrated a census and taxation system and a road system for the entire Empire

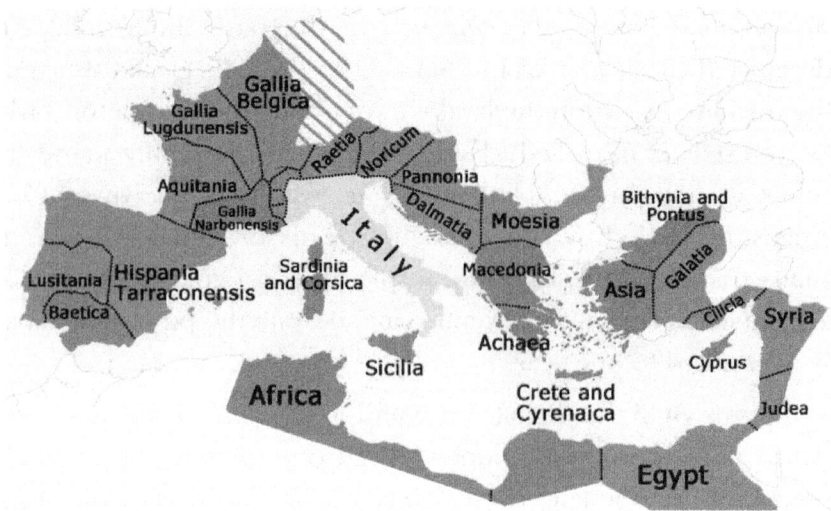

This map depicts the extent of the Roman Empire at the end of Augustus' reign.

https://commons.wikimedia.org/wiki/File:Roman_empire_14_AD_(provinces)_en.png

Despite three marriages, Augustus had only one child – Julia. His third wife, Livia, had two sons from her first husband – Tiberius and Drusus (the latter born about three months after she married Augustus). Drusus married Augustus' niece – Antonia – and their son Claudius became the fourth emperor of the Julio-Claudian dynasty.

Livia's older son Tiberius married Vipsania Agrippina, and they had a son: Drusus Julius Caesar. Romans had a habit of naming their sons after their brothers, which can get confusing. After eight years of happy marriage with Vipsania, Augustus asked Tiberius to divorce his wife and marry Augustus' daughter Julia – Tiberius' stepsister. That marriage was a disaster. Tiberius was still in love with Vipsania; Julia had been unfaithful to her previous husband, and she was unfaithful to Tiberius. Finally, Augustus charged his daughter with adultery and treason, declared her marriage to Tiberius void, and exiled her to a tiny island in the Tyrrhenian Sea. However, Augustus adopted two of her five children – Gaius Caesar and Lucius Caesar – as small children.

This left the question – who would be the next emperor? One of Augustus' biological grandsons? Or Tiberius – his stepson and former son-in-law? Augustus had all three educated and trained to succeed him – keeping his options open. Perhaps Tiberius assumed his stepfather would choose one of the grandsons, or perhaps he fell into one of his depressive episodes, but suddenly, after a promising political and military career, Tiberius dropped out of everything and retired to Rhodes.

After several years, both Gaius and Lucius died – leaving Tiberius as the only successor. Augustus legally adopted Tiberius in AD 4, and Tiberius adopted his nephew Germanicus. With his biological son Drusus and adopted son Germanicus, Tiberius now had two potential successors to the throne. Tiberius returned to Rome, picking up his political career. In AD 13, Tiberius became co-Princeps with Augustus – with equal powers – so Rome would have an uninterrupted rule whenever Augustus died.

Caesar Augustus died a year later in AD 14 and was promptly pronounced a god. The Senate met and validated Tiberius' position as Princeps (emperor). Tiberius deferred most decisions to the Senate, with little interest in the affairs of state – yet Rome mostly enjoyed peace and prosperity during his reign.

This bust of Tiberius was found in the ancient Roman city of Termes (in present-day Montejo de Tiermes, Province of Soria, Spain). https://commons.wikimedia.org/wiki/File:Tiberius_(M.A.N._Madrid)_01.jpg

Tiberius suffered from crushing and debilitating bouts of depression, not helped by his life's circumstances being – well, depressing. A dejected and disinterested leader, he only dipped into the state coffers for necessary things. On a high note, his lack of extravagance enabled him to leave an economic surplus to his successor.

Tiberius' nephew and adopted son Germanicus was highly popular, displaying brilliance in his military and political career; in AD 18, Tiberius gave him control over the Empire's eastern half –

implying he would be Tiberius' successor. Only a year later, he suddenly died, saying he'd been poisoned. Tiberius descended into depression again, giving his biological son Drusus his responsibilities, including sharing the tribunician power, while he retreated to southern Italy for two years. Then Drusus also suddenly died of mysterious circumstances (likely poisoned by Sejanus, a political rival) in AD 23.

With both Germanicus and Drusus dead, Tiberius had to quickly decide on a new heir. He adopted Germanicus' two sons – Nero (not the same Nero as the nefarious emperor) and Drusus. He then retired from Rome again, leaving the city under the charge of Sejanus – his Praetorian Prefect – unaware Sejanus had probably poisoned his son. While Tiberius fought the demons of depression and descended into debauchery in Capri, Sejanus, now consul, accused Nero of homosexuality and exiled him – where he died soon after. Sejanus imprisoned Drusus in the palace dungeon, starving him to death. The third son of Germanicus – Caligula – was saved when Tiberius summoned him to Capri, where he lived for six years.

After years of absence from Rome, Tiberius awakened to the growing threat of Sejanus and his crafty intrigues. Suddenly, in AD 31, Sejanus was arrested, executed by strangulation, then thrown down the Gemonian stairs, where the crowd tore his body to pieces. His wife committed suicide but first sent a letter to Tiberius, telling him Sejanus had poisoned Tiberius' son Drusus. Tiberius purged anyone in Rome suspected to have colluded with Sejanus.

Tiberius then retired back into seclusion, leaving the government to be run by the Senate, descending into paranoia. He did nothing about appointing a successor and died in AD 37, at age 77 – some whispered Caligula had smothered him.

Tiberius left his estate and titles to Caligula and Gemellus (his grandson by Drusus) – intending them to co-reign. Caligula immediately had the will nullified regarding Gemellus yet adopted the teenage boy. Although known by his nickname Caligula – meaning 'little boots" for the miniature military boots his father had made for him when he was a small child – his real name was Gaius Caesar Augustus Germanicus.

This cameo shows Caligula and Roma – a personification of Rome. By Andreas Praefcke - Self-photographed, Public Domain,
https://commons.wikimedia.org/w/index.php?curid=12437143

The Senate proclaimed Caligula emperor, hailed by Rome's people as their shining star. The first seven months of Caligula's reign seemed idyllic as he initiated reforms, reinstated elections, awarded the military with bonuses, granted tax relief, initiated construction projects, and entertained the citizens with extravagant games (which quickly emptied the treasury).

Then Caligula developed a serious illness. Cassio Dio said it was a brain fever – suggesting meningitis or encephalitis. By all accounts, he had a sudden personality change – turning diabolical. He was erratic, easily excitable, and narcissistic. Dio said he would impersonate the Roman gods and goddesses, believing himself to have a divine nature.

He probably had lifelong epilepsy – the Roman historian Suetonius said he had the "falling sickness" as a child; the symptoms improved in adolescence, but he would still have episodes of sudden weakness where he could not stand or sit up and would be mentally confused – suggesting atonic seizures. Suetonius also recorded sleep disruption – he could only sleep about three hours a night, tormented by nightmares.

After his near-fatal illness, Caligula became unhinged, paranoid of those around him, and given to sadistic cruelty. Suspecting his adopted son Gemellus of wishing his death, Caligula ordered him to commit suicide – helped by the palace guards. He exiled or killed his relatives, passing murders off as suicide. Treason trials and execution of statesmen became commonplace.

Did he really make his horse a priest? He doted on Incitatus, who lived in a marble stable with an ivory manger. Dio said he made the horse a priest, while Suetonius said he planned to make the horse a consul. Most like, he just made joking comments comparing the senators (with whom he had a running feud) unfavorably to his horse. But then again, this was Caligula, unbound by society's norms.

Caligula expanded the empire by taking over Mauretania, previously a client kingdom of Rome, by inviting King Ptolemy of Mauretania to Rome, executing him, and annexing Mauretania. He set Britain's conquest in motion before his early death at age 28.

After enduring his reign for less than four years, the Romans were ready for a change. The Praetorian Guard (and probably the Senate) conspired to kill him – stabbing him and his wife to death in

January AD 41 and smashing the head of his infant daughter against the wall.

This statue of Claudius is found in the Vatican Museum.
https://commons.wikimedia.org/wiki/File:ClaudiusJupiter.jpg

Tiberius Claudius Caesar Augustus Germanicus became the next emperor in AD 41 by default – he was the only adult male left in the family! Claudius survived the purges because of a disability – possibly Tourette's Syndrome. His knees were weak, he stumbled when he walked, he would laugh spontaneously at odd times, his head would shake from side to side when stressed, he drooled, he had a speech impediment, and he would make random, bizarre statements completely irrelevant to the matter at hand.

Caligula kept his uncle around for entertainment, encouraging his dinner guests to throw their olive pits at him. Even his mother called him a monstrosity. His symptoms decreased as he grew older, and he was recognized as a scholarly historian, eventually serving with Caligula as consul. While the Praetorian Guard was hunting down Caligula's wife and baby to murder, Claudius was hiding behind a curtain in the palace. Suddenly, a Praetorian Guard swept back the curtain, stared at Claudius, then knelt, telling the other guards, "This is Germanicus – our emperor!"

Claudius proved to be a conscientious and capable administrator, engaging in massive infrastructure projects throughout the empire: aqueducts, roads, ports, and canals. Despite the expenses of these projects, he recouped Caligula's debt disaster through well-balanced control of the treasury and centralizing the government. He expanded Rome's borders by launching 40,000 troops and several war elephants across the English Channel in AD 43, beginning the conquest of Britain, and bringing Thrace, Lycia, Judea, Austria, and Pamphylia under Rome's direct control. He extended Roman citizenship in the provinces. He was active in Rome's judicial system, even serving as a judge.

An avid womanizer, Claudius' love life was lethal. His first wife died on their wedding day. His third wife was a nymphomaniac who gave birth to a son and daughter – Britannicus and Octavia – during their short marriage. His fourth and final wife was his niece Agrippina, Caligula's sister.

Agrippina successfully manipulated Claudius to adopt Nero, her son from her first marriage, making him Claudius' successor over Britannicus. She arranged for Nero to marry his stepsister Octavia in AD 53. By that point, Claudius was having second thoughts about Agrippina and Nero, and was planning to elevate his biological son

Britannicus; Agrippina stopped all that by poisoning Claudius with mushrooms at a banquet, killing him in AD 54 at age 63.

Nero Claudius Caesar Augustus Germanicus became emperor of Rome at age 16 when Claudius died; his 13-year-old stepbrother Britannicus conveniently died – suddenly – three months later. Agrippina's plan to rule through her son failed – he banished her from the palace when she criticized his love affairs, then arranged for her to die in a shipwreck, which she survived, only to be stabbed to death in her villa. In the tradition of Caligula, her death was reported as a suicide.

In his first several years, guided by his tutor Seneca and his advisor Burrus, Nero gave the Senate more power, reduced taxes (he wanted to get rid of them altogether, but Seneca and Burrus explained why that wouldn't work), enhanced slave rights, and provided disaster assistance to cities in need. Through his competent generals, he oversaw victories in Armenia, Germany, and Britain, and promoted a successful expedition to discover the source of the Nile.

Of course, he wasn't personally involved in the military campaigns nor most politics. He gave his attention to the arts – singing, playing the lyre, dancing, acting, writing poetry, painting, and chariot racing. When the Olympic games were held in Rome, he added artistic competitions to the athletic contests and joined both competitions, winning all the ones he competed in, even a chariot race where he never finished (his chariot tipped over!)

After his tutor Brutus died in AD 62, his dark side took over. He forced Seneca to commit suicide, then panicked when he had to make decisions on his own. When his lover Poppaea became pregnant with his child, he divorced Octavia, sending her into exile and marrying Poppaea 12 days later. Nero and Poppaea then had Octavia killed in an overly hot bath.

Nero and Poppaea's daughter died at four months old, but two years later, Poppaea was pregnant again. In an intense argument, Nero kicked her in the belly – killing her and the unborn child. Nero was devastated, going into mourning, and giving her a state funeral. About a year later, he came upon a boy named Sporos, who may have been among the *puer deliciae* – male children with delicate features (usually slaves) abused by Roman men for their sexual pleasure. Sporos bore a remarkable resemblance to Poppaea. Nero had Sporos castrated and married him; Sporos accompanied his husband in public, wearing an empress' clothing.

Rome's fire of AD 64 destroyed two-thirds of the city.
https://commons.wikimedia.org/wiki/File:History_of_Nero_(1881)_(14586334218).jpg

A great fire erupted in Rome in AD 64, burning for over a week, destroying countless homes and temples. Most Roman historians of the day laid the blame on Nero, who needed to clear space for his Golden House project requiring at least 100 acres. To deflect suspicion, Nero blamed the Christians. Both Jews and pagans in Rome were drawn to Christianity through a revolutionary concept—an ideology of brotherly love instead of power. Nero rounded up the followers of *The Way*: crucifying them, throwing them to the wild beasts, or lighting his garden with their burning bodies. The apostle Peter was crucified, and Paul was decapitated.

After the fire, Nero's new building plan called for houses to be spaced apart from each other – not connected like townhouses as they had been, built from brick, not wood, and with a portico on the front. To cover the immense cost of rebuilding Rome, Nero devalued Roman currency, demanded tribute payments from the empire's provinces, and raised taxes.

Rome was growing weary of their despotic emperor. In AD 68, three provincial governors – Vindex, Galba, and Otho – rebelled against the heavy taxation, declaring Galba as the new emperor. Otho, Governor of Lusitania, bore a simmering rage against Nero for stealing his wife Poppaea – and then killing her. The Roman forces defeated Vindex's army in Gaul, but then the Roman legions also demanded a new emperor.

When the Praetorian Guard turned against Nero, he left town, intending to sail to the eastern provinces with his boy-wife Sporos, but he didn't get far beyond Rome's walls – his army refused to take him anywhere. Nero realized his only option was suicide. He ordered his servants to dig his grave but then lost his nerve, asking one of his companions to go first. No one volunteered. Still unable to kill himself, he asked his secretary to stab him. Nero died at age 30 on June 9, 68 – the end of the Julio-Claudian Dynasty.

Tacitus described the following year – the Year of the Four Emperors – as "a period rich in disasters ... even in peace, full of horrors." Once again, Rome was embroiled in a bitter civil war. Vindex, the orchestrator of the rebellion, had committed suicide, but on the night of Nero's death, the Senate proclaimed Galba as their new emperor.

Galba faced the immediate threat of Nymphidius Sabinus, the Prefect of the Praetorian Guard, who had his own ambitions for being emperor. Nymphidius had convinced his men to abandon

Nero, but when Nymphidius married Nero's boy-wife Sporos and tried to make himself emperor, his own men killed him.

Galba had a reputation for greed and cruelty - as he marched toward Rome through Spain and Gaul, he decimated or heavily fined any cities in his path that questioned his right to rule them. After entering Rome, he canceled Nero's reforms and executed distinguished citizens without trial, based on trivial suspicions. His rule lasted seven months.

The Roman legions in Germany refused to swear loyalty to Galba - proclaiming their own governor - Vitellius - as emperor. Meanwhile, the Praetorian Guard staged a coup d'état, killing Galba in the Forum and putting forward their candidate - Otho - for emperor (who had bribed them well). With great relief, the Senate approved Otho, who wasn't expected to be a brutish despot.

Otho took the boy Sporos (who resembled his late wife Poppaea) for himself and set to work stabilizing Rome - finding that leading a coup was far easier than putting the pieces together afterward. Within weeks, he learned Vitellius was marching from Germany toward Rome. Vitellius dismissed Otho's offer to share the empire. Although the omens were against him, Otho marched north with his legions to defend Italy's borders, but he was too late. Vitellius' forces had crossed the Alps and were already in northern Italy. Vitellius won the ensuing battle, the Roman soldiers quickly switched to his side, and Otho committed suicide - ending his three-month reign.

As soon as the Senate heard of Otho's suicide, they recognized Vitellius as emperor while he marched toward Rome. He enlarged the Praetorian Guard by installing his loyal soldiers from Germany, then began a succession of celebratory banquets and triumphal parades. He also disposed of his rivals by forcing them to participate in cruel games and gladiator shows. He planned to torture and kill the hapless Sporos in a reenactment of the Rape of Proserpina, but the boy killed himself first.

His lavish feasting and parades emptied the treasury, so he resorted to convincing citizens to name him as their heir, then killed them and collected their estates. After three months of gluttony and games, reality struck – in the form of a new contender. Egypt, Judea, and Syria announced their own emperor: Titus Flavius Vespasianus – the hero legate who led the British Conquest in AD 43.

Leaving his son Titus to deal with the Jewish Rebellion in Judea, Vespasian was on his way to Italy when the legions in Switzerland, Germany, Austria, and the Balkans also acclaimed him as their emperor. Before Vespasian arrived in Italy, the northern legions crossed the Alps into northern Italy, scoring an overwhelming victory over Vitellius, who was decapitated and his body thrown into the Tiber, thus ending the Year of Four Emperors with Vespasian on the throne – the founder of the Flavian Dynasty.

Despite the chaos of the Julio-Claudian Dynasty and the Year of the Four Kings, the rest of the empire was experiencing peace – at least, more law and order than the provinces around the Mediterranean had enjoyed for millennia. The *Pax Romana* or Roman Peace extended from around 27 BC (when Augustus Caesar's reign began) to AD 180 (when Marcus Aurelius died). With a central government, common languages (Latin and Greek), and an excellent and extensive road system, the empire could surge ahead with unprecedented trade, economic growth, engineering feats, and cultural growth. Travel was relatively safe due to Roman legions stationed around the empire discouraging bandits on land and pirates at sea.

The *Pax Romana* immensely affected the spread of Christianity. The New Testament records that Jesus was born during the reign of Augustus, and his teaching ministry took place under Tiberius' reign. The Apostle Paul's missionary journeys throughout much of the Roman Empire took place under Claudius and Nero, enabled by the Pax Romana. Rome was generally tolerant of other religions, and Christians had been only sporadically targeted for persecution until the last few years of Nero's reign. As a Roman citizen, Paul appealed to Caesar – Nero – when the Jews arrested him. His appeal was granted, and he was taken to Rome, where he stayed in his own rented house for two years in the custody of the Praetorian Guard, developing friendships that extended into Nero's household.

Chapter 11: The Flavians and the Antonines

Although cursed by a horrific volcanic eruption, another fire in Rome, and a plague, the Flavian Dynasty restored stability and dignity to Rome after the Year of the Four Emperors' violent power struggle. It was followed by the Antonine Dynasty, known for stability in the frontiers, good emperors, prosperity, uncontested successions, and flourishing arts.

Titus Flavius Vespasianus - founder of the Flavian Dynasty - rose from modest origins to bring Rome back to a place of honor, strength, and cohesion during his ten-year reign. His road to power came through distinguished service in the military, capturing the admiration of his forces who proclaimed him emperor in the chaos following Nero's fall. Before becoming emperor, he was a driving force in Britain's invasion, then served as proconsul in Africa - that didn't go so swimmingly - the people bombarded him with turnips, frustrated at his tight budget.

Nero appointed him in AD 67 to crush the Great Jewish Revolt - a rebellion of the commoners against both the Jewish and Roman ruling class. In AD 66, Jewish Zealots attacked Roman citizens; the Roman governor Gessius Florus retaliated by plundering the

Temple in Jerusalem. The outraged Jews massacred 6000 Roman soldiers, and that's when Nero sent Vespasian to destroy the Jewish forces and punish the citizens. Vespasian and his son Titus slaughtered or sold into slavery about 10,000 Jews in Caesarea and Galilee, and the rebel Jewish forces fled north to Jerusalem.

Vespasian returned to Rome to become the new emperor, but Titus besieged Jerusalem for seven months, starving the people. Three decades earlier, Jesus had wept over Jerusalem, prophesying the siege. Titus breached the walls, burned the city – including the temple, and leveled it to the ground. One million Jews died in Judea, and 60,000 were taken as slaves to Rome to build the Colosseum. The temple in Jerusalem was never rebuilt.

One of Vespasian's first tasks as emperor was to raise money to recoup what had been lost from Nero's extravagance, to repair damage to buildings and infrastructure from a year of civil war, and to begin new construction projects on temples, a theater, and the Colosseum. He reclaimed public land and raised taxes, even placing a tax on public toilets, inducing the citizens to mockingly name urinals *vespasiano* after him.

The Colosseum was built in the Flavian Dynasty to host games, gladiator competitions, and wild animal fights.
https://commons.wikimedia.org/wiki/File:Colosseum_in_Rome-April_2007-1-_copie_2B.jpg

In AD 70, Vespasian initiated construction on the Colosseum – the largest ancient amphitheater still standing in the world – in the center of Rome, just east of the Forum. It was finished in AD 80 by his son Titus; his second son Domitian made further modifications during his reign. It was known as the Flavian Amphitheater and used for games, gladiator battles, and wild animal fights. During Vespasian's reign, General Agricola expanded and consolidated Rome's province in Britain, thrusting north into Scotland.

Vespasian was known for his common sense and earthy humor. When he was dying from persistent diarrhea, he quipped, "Dear me, I think I'm becoming a god," poking fun at the Romans' custom of elevating their emperors to god status upon their death. He died in AD 79 at 69, and his son Titus assumed the throne – the first time a Roman emperor was succeeded by his biological son.

Titus Caesar Vespasianus was popular and admired for his military and administrative competence along with his reforms, such as outlawing treason trials, which were being used as witch hunts to eliminate rivals. But most of Titus' brief two-year reign was spent in disaster management: three horrific catastrophes struck Italy in quick succession just two months after he ascended the throne.

On August 24, AD 79, Mount Vesuvius exploded – shooting ash and pumice ten miles into the stratosphere, which then rained down on Pompeii. Most citizens fled, but about 2000 sheltered in their homes – but worse peril awaited them the following morning. The volcano engulfed the town of Herculaneum in a lethal cloud of asphyxiating gas and hot ash, then buried it under 60 feet of mud. The same toxic gas killed those still in Pompeii, then 14 feet of ash and pumice covered the city.

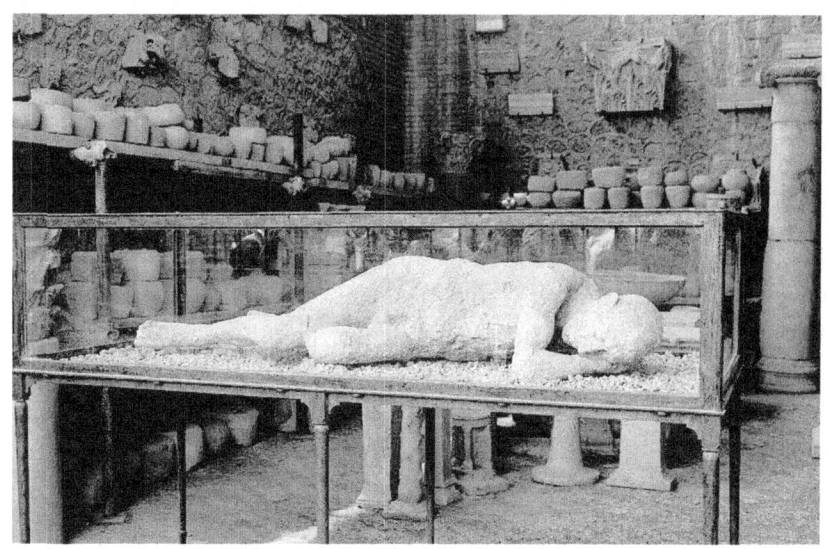

The bodies of Vesuvius' victims in Pompeii were covered in ash, which hardened into a shell, preserving them for almost two millennia. Beginning in 1863, plaster was poured into the hardened shells, forming casts of the victims.
https://commons.wikimedia.org/wiki/File:Pompeii_casts_18.jpg

Vespasian's friend, Pliny the Elder – author, naturalist, philosopher, and naval commander – was an eyewitness to the eruption, along with his 18-year-old nephew Pliny the Younger. Pliny was stationed with the Roman fleet at Misenum, across the Bay of Naples from Mount Vesuvius, and his nephew wrote of the volcanic cloud rising high and extending out in several branches – like a pine tree. Pliny the Elder organized a rescue mission for Stabiae. As they sailed across the bay, pumice and cinders fell on the ship. They rescued some survivors, but just as they were leaving, they were enveloped by hot toxic gasses which asphyxiated Pliny.

Titus appointed two former consuls to assess and coordinate relief work, donating a generous sum from the state treasury for the victims. He visited the area twice, and while on his second visit in the spring of AD 80, Rome caught fire again, burning for three days and nights, destroying Agrippa's Pantheon, the Theater of Pompey, the Temple of Jupiter, and much more. Titus compensated those who lost their homes or businesses. While the fire was burning in Rome, a lethal epidemic broke out in the countryside, killing 10,000 a day.

Titus celebrated the grand opening of the Flavian Amphitheater (Colosseum) in AD 80, with 100 days of entertainment and games. He also unveiled the new public Baths of Titus just next to the Colosseum. After dedicating these two edifices, he headed for the Sabine territory, but suddenly fell ill, developed a high fever, and died – cut short in the prime of life after only two years as emperor.

When Titus's younger brother Domitian ascended the throne as the last Flavian emperor, he squelched hopes he would follow in his father and brother's footsteps. Rude and tyrannical toward the senators, he stripped their power. He exhibited odd behaviors, disappearing into a room to catch flies and pierce them with a needle, leading the people to joke, "Who was the emperor with today?" "No one! No even a fly."

But Domitian ran the empire with efficiency – tending to micromanage. He enforced rigorous taxes to cover the cost of the two lavish palaces he built for himself – one in Rome and the other in the Alban Hills, and construction of the Stadium of Domitian for athletic competitions. Toward the end of his fifteen-year reign, he steadily grew paranoid, executing a least twenty senators for treason or corruption. His paranoia was not misplaced – he was assassinated in AD 96 – stabbed in the groin – by Stephanus, a freed slave, in a plot devised by his chamberlain Parthenius, ending the Flavian Dynasty.

On the day Domitian was assassinated, the Senate announced Marcus Cocceius Nerva as Rome's next emperor – ushering in the Antonine Dynasty and the first of the "five good emperors" who brought order, balance, and wealth to Rome.

Why did the Senate choose the elderly Nerva? Perhaps simply because he was older and in ill health – he would be a "placeholder" while the Senate figured out who they really wanted. To his credit, in his 15 months as emperor, Nerva relieved the tax burden, passed economic reforms, granted land allotments to the poor, curtailed the extravagant sacrifices and entertainment draining the treasury, and completed the public works projects initiated by the Flavians.

Nerva did nothing to investigate and punish Domitian's assassins – in the struggle, Domitian had stabbed his killer Stephanus, who died with him. Maybe Nerva feared the conspirators would come after him. Finally, the frustrated Praetorian Guard held him hostage until he agreed to arrest and prosecute the chamberlain and others involved in the plot.

In AD 97, he adopted Marcus Ulpius Traianus as his heir and successor; six months later, he suffered a stroke and died soon after.

Trajan served as the second of the "five good emperors" of the Antonine Dynasty. https://commons.wikimedia.org/w/index.php?curid=1954744

The new emperor Trajan was born in Spain to Roman parents. Although unrelated, Nerva adopted him, making him his heir due to Trajan's illustrious military career – Nerva desperately needed the support of the military. Trajan had also served as a governor in northern Europe and consul of Rome. Before becoming emperor, Trajan became guardian to his cousins Hadrian and Paulina, whose parents had died.

As emperor, Trajan removed much of the Senate's power but made governmental decisions that the Senate would likely have made anyway, earning the reputation of a virtuous autocrat and a role model of moderation. He was notable for appointing at least fourteen Greek senators to Rome's Senate – making it more representative of the empire's provincial population and helping alleviate simmering tensions with the eastern half of the empire.

Trajan was a soldier more than anything else, and his primary concern was expanding the empire's borders. After two wars, he conquered Dacia (in modern Romania), turning it into a Roman province. He annexed the Nabataean kingdom of the northwestern Arabian Desert after its Bedouin client-king died, consolidating it with Jordan, southern Levant, and the Sinai Peninsula to form the Roman province of Arabia Petraea. In his last military campaign, he annexed Armenia and Babylon as provinces

With the plunder gained from his military victories, Trajan renovated the Circus Maximus and expanded the Forum, but also formed a welfare program for the orphans and poor children of Italy, providing food and education. He hosted three months of games at the Colosseum with five million spectators watching chariot racing, gladiator contests, and fighting beasts – 11,000 gladiator slaves and criminals died.

While on his final campaign in Mesopotamia in AD 117, Trajan suffered heatstroke. On his deathbed, he named Hadrian as his adopted son and successor – although rumors swirled that his wife Plotina forged the document.

This bronze figure of Hadrian is in the Israel Museum.
https://commons.wikimedia.org/wiki/File:Hadrian-
_An_Emperor_Cast_in_Bronze,_Israel_Museum_(27801269805).jpg

Caesar Traianus Hadrianus' twenty-year reign raised the Roman Empire to its greatest height. Hadrian spent half his reign traveling outside Rome, ensuring proficient provincial administration and army discipline. In 122, he built the 73-mile Hadrian's Wall in Britain, extending completely across the island from the Irish Sea to the North Sea, protecting Britain from the fierce tattooed Picts of Scotland. Throughout Asia, Africa, and Europe, he built monuments and cities while improving infrastructure and roads. In Rome, he rebuilt the Pantheon, repaired Trajan's Forum, and constructed Roman baths.

In 132, Hadrian rebuilt Jerusalem, provoking the Jews by building a temple to Jupiter just where the sacred Jewish temple once stood, which spurred the Bar-Kochba Revolt. During the fierce war, 580,000 Jews were killed, and 1000 towns were razed. He renamed the province Palaestina, evicted the Jews, burned the Torah, and outlawed the Jewish faith.

After putting down the revolt, Hadrian's health failed, and he retired permanently to Rome. Months before his death in 138, Hadrian adopted Antoninus Pius as his son and successor, who then adopted Lucius Verus and Marcus Aurelius.

With the most peaceful reign of any Roman Emperor, Antoninus Pius had no stunning military conquest, no extravagances, no oddities – other than not being odd. He didn't travel around like Hadrian – he just stayed in Italy and managed the empire as a sensible model of respectability. His long and happy marriage to Faustina produced four children, but only their youngest daughter, Faustina the Younger, lived to see him crowned as emperor. She married her cousin Marcus Aurelius – who had been adopted by Antoninus – and together, they had 13 children with two sets of twins.

Before becoming emperor, Antoninus had excelled as a proficient governor of Asia. As emperor, he was a shrewd political operator with a keen financial sense, leaving the treasury with a surplus. He built the Temple of Antoninus and Faustina in honor of his wife, which was later converted to a Catholic church in the fifth century. He rebuilt the ancient Pons Sublicius bridge over the Tiber, and other bridges, roads, and aqueducts.

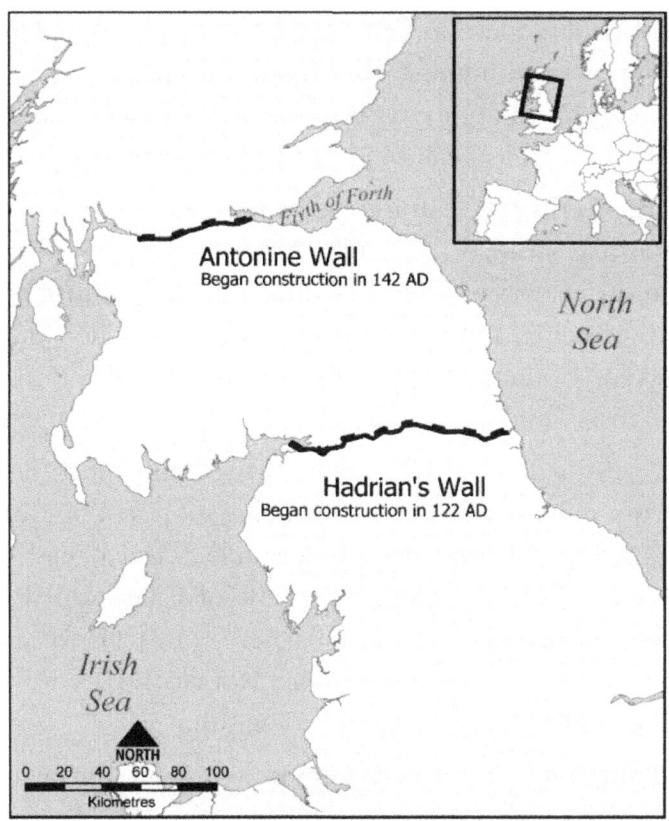

Hadrian's Wall was built during Hadrian's reign and the Antonine Wall during Antoninus' rule.
https://commons.wikimedia.org/wiki/File:Hadrians_Wall_map.png

Although Antoninus remained in Italy, his Numidian general Quintus Lollius Urbicus scored a modest victory when he invaded Scotland, taking additional territory and building the Antonine Wall 100 miles north of Hadrian's Wall. Antoninus was the first Roman ruler to send a diplomatic mission to China (during its Han Dynasty), which went down in Chinese records. Antoninus died in 161, leaving the empire to his two adopted sons – Marcus Aurelius and Lucius Verus – to co-rule.

Marcus Aurelius – a Stoic philosopher – wrote *Meditations*: insights on meaningful life and human behavior. He ascended to the throne with his adoptive brother Lucius Verus – the first time

Rome had dual emperors. Verus wasn't scholarly like Marcus – he preferred sports and hunting. In this awkward arrangement, Marcus Aurelius held more authority, but together they continued leading the empire through its peak of power and prosperity.

The pair were almost immediately tested when King Vologases IV of Parthia invaded Armenia. With no military experience, Marcus and Lucius sent Marcus Statius Priscus, governor of Britain, to retake Armenia, but that ended in disaster. Then the Syrians rebelled. One of them needed to head east to deal with things, but who?

Lucius was sent – he had been partying too much and would benefit from military discipline, plus being more cut out for warfare than the erudite Marcus. Lucius leisurely traveled east, feasting, hunting, and visiting the pleasure resorts of Cilicia and Pamphylia before finally reaching Antioch, where he had to assume a modicum of military discipline. The Roman forces were just as dissolute – drinking, gambling, and going soft.

The temporarily reformed Lucius led them through training exercises, marching or running with them on foot. He ordered his men to build a shipping canal on the Orontes River to bypass a waterfall – the construction exposed a massive 18-foot-long earthenware coffin holding the remains of a giant. In the middle of the war, he traveled to Ephesus to marry 13-year-old Anna Lucilla – daughter of Marcus Aurelius.

The Roman generals captured Armenia, and while Lucius was appointing a new king, the troublesome Parthians invaded Osroene, east of Syria. In 165, Roman forces marched on Mesopotamia, chasing the Parthians to the Tigris, where their general desperately jumped in the river, swimming downstream to a cave where he took refuge. Rome triumphantly took control of all western Mesopotamia, and Lucius returned to Rome and back to partying, hailed as a war hero, although his astute generals had done the real work.

The Antonine Plague – a pandemic of either smallpox or measles – swept the Roman Empire beginning in 165, brought back from the east by the military. Rome lost 2000 souls a day, at least five million died throughout the empire, and the Roman army was decimated. Lucius fell ill, dying in early 169, leaving Marcus as sole emperor.

While Lucius had been fighting in the east, Marcus was resisting invasions of the Germanic tribes, the Iranian Iazyges tribe, and the Costoboci of the Carpathian Mountains. Marcus pushed backed some invasions, but other times the tribes settled in Roman provinces.

Marcus was experienced and adept in legal affairs and conscientious about freeing slaves and providing guardianship for orphans. He diplomatically asked the Senate permission for funding and spoke of his palace as belonging to the people. His death in 180 brought an end to the Pax Romana, as his son Commodus ascended the throne. In the words of Cassius Dio, Rome descended "from a kingdom of gold to one of iron and rust."

Commodus – Rome's new 18-year-old emperor – was a sociopathic megalomaniac. Cassius Dio, an acquaintance, was kinder, saying he didn't have an evil nature but was easily manipulated by his companions, who introduced him to a cruel and indecent lifestyle. Having co-ruled with Marcus Aurelius for two years before his father's death, he had acquired valuable military and administrative experience. But when Marcus Aurelius died, Commodus returned to his reckless and fawning friends, rejecting his father's Stoic asceticism.

His first three years were unremarkable – the empire was relatively peaceful, and his father's advisers kept things running smoothly. But then, it happened. His older sister Lucilla conspired to assassinate him, perhaps concerned his erratic behavior would destroy Rome. The assassins bungled things, and Commodus survived, executing his would-be killers and exiling and later executing Lucilla.

Commodus became paranoid, imaging treachery and plots all around him. He wasn't off-base – conspiracies to kill him continued throughout his reign. Two men – Perennis and Cleander – murdered his chamberlain. Unaware of their involvement, Commodus appointed Perennis as his Praetorian Prefect and Cleander as his new chamberlain. Disinterested in administration, Commodus gave Perennis charge over most of his duties – which Perennis conducted competently, that is, until he was named in a plot to overthrow Commodus and executed.

Perennis' successor Aebutianus was also accused – by Cleander – of plotting to kill Commodus, and after Aebutianus' execution, Cleander took over as Prefect, enriching himself by selling coveted political positions to the highest bidder. Unfortunately for Cleander, a food shortage hit Rome, and the man responsible for grain – Dionysius – blamed Cleander, who hid in Commodus' palace from an angry mob. On the urging of his mistress Marcia, Commodus beheaded Cleander, handing his head on a pike to the mob, then had the mutilated bodies of Cleander's wife and children dragged through the streets.

Commodus was obsessed with playing gladiator, striding into the arena to fight men and animals. He especially enjoyed fighting disabled people. Gladiator contests didn't always involve killing; often, it was a competition to demonstrate which fighter had the superior skill. But the bloodthirsty Commodus always demanded gory death – whether he was watching a contest or fighting himself. Whenever Commodus showed up in the arena, the state had to pay a fee of a million sesterces, driving the struggling economy toward collapse.

Commodus wore a lion skin, impersonating the god Hercules.
https://commons.wikimedia.org/wiki/File:Commodus_as_Hercules_(detail)_-
_Palazzo_dei_Conservatori_-_Musei_Capitolini_-_Rome_2016_(2).jpg

Commodus believed he was a god – he pressured the Senate to declare him the incarnate Hercules, son of Zeus, and walked around impersonating Hercules in a lion-hide cloak. After receiving a cold response, he massacred most of the Senators and other administrators on New Year's Eve, intending to be the sole dictator. In the words of Dio, the Romans felt "Commodus was a greater curse to the Romans than any pestilence or crime." His mistress Maria colluded with others to kill him, putting poison in his food, which he vomited up. As he was cleaning off the vomit in the bath, his wrestling partner Narcissus choked him to death, ending the reign of madness in March 193.

Just as the Julio-Claudian Dynasty ended with the Year of Four Emperors, the Antonine Dynasty ended with the Year of Five Emperors. Pertinax, a senator who had served as Proconsul of Africa, was chosen as emperor by Commodus' assassins – basically because he was one of the few nobles still alive after Commodus' purge. Pertinax was a disciplined administrator, but he offended the Praetorian Guard by failing to give the usual monetary gifts at his accession and then imposed stricter discipline over them; the disgruntled Praetorian Guard killed him, then enriched themselves by auctioning the position of emperor.

The highest bidder was the affluent senator Didius Julianus, who had served as Proconsul of Africa after Pertinax. Hated by the people for buying his position, his reign as emperor lasted two months. He was overcome and killed by Septimius Severus, a governor in central Europe, who expected to become emperor. Before that could happen, Septimius had to get rid of his rivals.

Pescennius Niger, governor of Syria, declared himself emperor with the backing of the eastern legions. Severus appointed Clodius Albinus (another contender for emperor) as temporary Caesar while Severus was in the east fighting Niger. Severus defeated Niger, decapitating him, then turned on Albinus, defeating and killing him. After purging his rivals' followers, Severus became sole emperor and the founder of the Severan Dynasty. Although the new dynasty had some successful emperors, it would never again experience the wealth, power, and stability of the Antonine Dynasty.

Chapter 12: The Severan Dynasty

An African family of Semitic-Phoenician descent headed up the new dynasty in Rome. The cruel tyrant Commodus was dead, and Severus had risen to take his place, founder of the Severan Dynasty. Five Severan emperors ruled the Roman Empire for 47 years, from AD 193-235, with an interlude of one non-Severan emperor. The empire fell into decline on their watch, due to incessant barbarian invasions, conflict with the Praetorian Guard prohibiting strong sovereignty, unstable Severan family dynamics, and constant political turmoil rocking Rome.

Septimius Severus was born into a Phoenician family in northern Africa. With exemplary military service, he rose through the ranks until he became governor of Upper Pannonia in central Europe. His Syrian wife Julia Domna was actively involved in politics while he was emperor – unusual for Roman women who ruled through their husbands or sons.

In 195, attempting to gain credibility with the Roman people, Severus had himself posthumously adopted by Marcus Aurelius, so he could claim lineage from the respected emperor of the Antonine Dynasty. He then gave his older son, Caracalla, the imperial rank of

Caesar and pronounced him Latin (ethnically, he was north African and Semitic).

The Severan Tondo, circa AD 200, depicts the African-Phoenician Severus with his Syrian wife Julia Domna, and two sons, Geta and Caracalla. Geta's face was blotted out as part of the damnatio memoriae (damnation of memory).
https://commons.wikimedia.org/wiki/File:Portrait_of_family_of_Septimius_Severus_-_Altes_Museum_-_Berlin_-_Germany_2017.jpg

Severus triumphed against the Parthians, sacking their capital city and extending Rome's borders to the Tigris River. He expanded and fortified Rome's Arabian Provence and rebuilt Hadrian's Wall in northern Britain. In Africa, he fought the Garamantes (Berber tribes from the Sahara desert), conquering their capital Garama in Libya and expanding the Roman desert frontier between Libya and Tunisia.

His relationship with the Senate was frosty, having seized power without their blessing and making himself a military dictator, but the military and the common people admired him for bringing stability after the horrors of Commodus' reign. Severus executed many senators on charges of corruption or conspiracy, installing his supporters in their place.

Throughout the Severan Dynasty, sporadic persecution of Jews and Christians took place – mainly because they persisted in monotheistic worship – refusing to embrace the Roman pantheon of gods. Most of Rome's conquered people were already polytheistic, so they would include the Roman deities while still worshiping their own gods. In return, the Romans would even build temples for foreign deities in the provinces and occasionally incorporated the gods of other people into their pantheon.

But the Jews and Christians were a different story. They only worshiped the god of Abraham, Isaac, and Jacob. They refused to offer sacrifices to Roman gods or participate in Roman religious festivals – which seem disloyal to the Romans, testing their religious tolerance. Since the Jews had a monotheistic history going back for millennia, the Romans usually gave them a pass. But Christianity was a new cult in Rome's eyes – an illegal superstition. They thought that holy communion was literal cannibalism and drinking blood.

As for Severus, his Christian doctor had successfully treated him through a severe illness, so he was personally not against Christianity and even protected some of his Christian acquaintances. The persecutions mostly took place at the local level – not by imperial edict – in the provinces. Christians were thrown to the wild beasts, beheaded, and thrown into scalding baths. At least two bishops of Rome were executed in the later Severan Dynasty.

When his oldest son Caracalla was ten years old, Severus proclaimed him as co-emperor and *Pontifex Maximus* (high priest) on the day Severus celebrated his triumph over the Parthian

Empire. This was mostly honorary until the boy was old enough to assist his father in ruling, but it paved the way for an easier succession. In 209, Severus made his younger son Geta co-emperor; thus, Rome had three emperors reigning together for two years until Severus died. After he died in 211, the brothers ruled together – unsuccessfully.

Caracalla's real name was Lucius Septimius Bassianus, but he liked wearing hoodies, even when he slept, so he was nicknamed Caracalla after the Gallic hooded tunic. His father had intended him to rule jointly with his younger brother Publius Septimius Geta – but sharing power ended in failure and tragedy. When their father was alive, Caracalla was Severus' military second-in-command, while Geta oversaw the administrative and bureaucratic end of things. But even then, rivalry and antagonism simmered between the brothers.

The brothers had been with their father in Britain when he died, but on their return journey to Rome with their father's ashes, they were either arguing or avoiding each other – staying in different lodging and never sharing a meal. Their mother, Julia Domna, who had been their father's confidante and key advisor, desperately tried to mediate – to no avail.

When they got back to Rome, they lived and worked in separate sections of the palace – even their servants could not cross to the other's side of the building. They were petrified of assassination by the other – always keeping bodyguards around them and only meeting when their mother was present. Julia Domna was the stabilizing force in their tense standoff, acting as a go-between and collaborating cooperatively with the generals and courtiers.

Julia Domna was torn between her two sons, Caracalla and Geta.
https://commons.wikimedia.org/wiki/File:Julia_Domna_Glyptothek_Munich_354.jpg

The brothers even proposed splitting the empire in half – each ruling their own section – but their mother talked them out of it, crying, "as you say, the Propontic Gulf separates the continents. But your mother, how would you parcel her? How am I to be torn and ripped asunder for the pair of you?"

Herodian wrote that she clasped both in her arms, with tears streaming down her face. The meeting adjourned, and the brothers walked out – each to their side of the palace. Their antipathy grew, and in every joint decision they had to make, the brothers were diametrically opposed. They each tried to devise ways to poison the other, but both took precautions. Finally, Caracalla produced a plan.

He told his mother he was ready to reconcile with Geta, asking her to summon him to her apartment, so they could meet with her. Domna persuaded Geta to come, but once he was inside her room, the centurions suddenly rushed toward Geta and stabbed him. Geta staggered toward his mother, falling into her embrace, as the soldiers continued to run him through, even cutting Domna, soaked in her son's blood.

Caracalla fled to the Praetorian camp, telling the troops that Geta had just attempted to kill him and had been killed in the struggle. After he heavily bribed the praetorians (and emptying the treasury), the Praetorian Guard proclaimed Geta an enemy and Caracalla sole emperor. Cassius Dio said everyone that lived on Geta's side of the palace was immediately butchered, even women and babies, and altogether 20,000 of Geta's soldiers, servants, and supporters were slain. Domna – wife and mother of emperors – was forbidden to weep for Geta; not even in private could she express her sorrow for her dead son.

Not satisfied with killing his brother, Caracalla set out to erase Geta's existence in the *damnatio memoriae* (damnation of memory). His name was blotted from documents, his image on paintings, coins, and statues was destroyed. With his brother erased, Caracalla survived through the loyalty of his troops, but that would not last long. Before he was 30, his sins would catch up with him, and he would be betrayed.

Caracalla ruled jointly with Geta, until he assassinated his brother, taking the throne completely for himself.
https://commons.wikimedia.org/wiki/File:Caracalla_MAN_Napoli_Inv6033_n06.jpg

Caracalla found administrative affairs tedious – his brother had managed those things before, and now his mother Domna assumed much of the everyday running of the empire. Caracalla gave his attention to military affairs – as he always had done.

When he was 14, Caracalla's parents had forced him into an arranged marriage to Fulvia Plautilla, whom he hated. They had one daughter, but then her father was executed for treachery, and Plautilla was sent into exile. Caracalla ordered her strangled after his father died. Neither Geta nor Caracalla had a son to continue the dynasty.

Caracalla passed the Antonine Constitution, extending Roman citizenship to all free men in the Roman Empire; previously, citizenship had mostly been limited to those living in or born in Italy. Cassius Dio felt Caracalla did this for tax revenue – only citizens had to pay inheritance taxes. Caracalla needed to refill the treasury to pay the military well and keep their support. Caracalla also constructed the Baths of Caracalla and introduced a new currency – the antoninianus – a coin worth two denarii.

Caracalla left Rome within a year after his brother's assassination – never to return. He saw himself as a modern-day Alexander the Great, affecting his style and implementing his battle strategies. Caracalla headed north to push back the Alemanni (Germanic tribes). Through strengthening frontier fortifications, he effectively blocked any further invasions for two decades.

The following year, he toured the eastern provinces, reaching Egypt in December 2015, where he had a score to settle with the Alexandrians, who had produced a mocking satire of his claims that Geta was killed in self-dense. Arriving in Alexandria, he reaped his revenge by slaughtering the dignitaries welcoming him at the gate and plundering the city.

In April of 2017, he was traveling through what is now southern Turkey and stopped to urinate, when, suddenly, one of his soldiers, Justin Martialis, stabbed him to death. Martialis was instantly killed by the other soldiers, but the Praetorian Prefect Macrinus, with the military behind him, declared himself emperor three days later. The Senate, far away in Rome, was helpless to do anything, although they were thanking the gods that Macrinus had gotten rid of the homicidal Caracalla.

At the time of Caracalla's death at age 29, Julia Domna was in Antioch, managing his correspondence. Suffering from breast cancer, she committed suicide on hearing the news. Her feelings for

Caracalla were complicated – she hated him for killing Geta, yet he was still her son, and part of her loved him anyway. Through him, she had power over the empire. Now she had lost her reason for living. Macrinus would be the emperor of the interlude, but within months, Domna's sister Julia Maesa would restore the Severan Dynasty in 218.

Marcus Opellius Macrinus never visited Rome during his 14-month reign, choosing to rule from Antioch. Born in Caesarea, he was African, like the Severan family, but of Berber descent, with a pierced ear, which the historian and senator Cassius Dio found unseemly.

Macrinus had two military issues to address immediately: finishing the war that Caracalla had started in Parthia and dealing with an Armenian rebellion. He took care of both situations with diplomatic negotiations, then turned his attention to Rome's internal affairs, which were in disarray – especially the dire financial straits.

He reversed Caracalla's fiscal policies – something had to be done about the exorbitant pay for soldiers that had drained the treasury. Unwilling to rock the boat with his current soldiers, he permitted them to retain the same inflated pay, but newly-enlisted men received the salary paid in Severus' time. Macrinus' goal was economic stability, but it angered the military. Even though only new recruits were affected by reduced pay, the veterans guessed that it wouldn't be long before their own pay was reduced.

Julia Domna's sister, Julia Maesa, was still living in the imperial court in Rome, where both her husband and daughter had reached senatorial rank. Macrinus sent her back to Syria. Her hometown in Emesa, Syria was next to a Roman military base, and her family socialized with some of their former friends from Rome, along with some new friends, forming a tight bond with the Roman legion.

Her grandson Elagabalus bore a strong resemblance to his second cousin, Caracalla, and Maesa capitalized on this by spreading rumors he was the lovechild of Caracalla and her daughter Soaemias. She also generously spread her immense wealth among key military leaders and played on their dissatisfaction with Macrinus, instigating a coup. The Roman legion took the boy into their camp one night, wrapped him in purple, and declared him their legitimate emperor of Severan lineage: son of Caracalla and grandson of Severus. Other legions began abandoning Macrinus and defecting to Elagabalus.

Macrinus marched on Syria, but his army defected to Elagabalus, and Macrinus had to escape to Antioch. Elagabalus' army (formerly Macrinus') marched on Antioch, fighting the Praetorian Guard protecting Macrinus. The Praetorian Guard was prevailing, but suddenly Maesa and her daughter Soaemias charged toward the fray in their chariot, leaping out to rally the men and turn the tide of the battle. Elagabalus' army roared at the sight of the women and routed the Praetorian Guard. Macrinus fled, hiding out in Antioch, shaving his beard and hair to disguise himself. He slipped out of Antioch, trying to escape Elagabalus, but he was caught and executed in Cappadocia.

Elagabalus became emperor at age 14, shocking Rome with controversial behaviors.

Rome now had a 14-year-old emperor, the child of Arab parents from Syria. His grandmother had been promoting him as Caracalla's bastard son; upon ascending the throne, he took Caracalla's official name: Marcus Aurelius Antoninus. His name Elagabalus came from his position as high priest of Elagabal – the sun god in Syria. He reigned for less than four years, scandalizing Rome with weird behaviors, sexual promiscuity, and strange religious customs. The woman who put him on the throne eventually ripped his life away when he was only 18.

The Senate acknowledged Elagabalus as emperor, along with his claims to be Caracalla's son. Macrinus was expunged from the record – Elagabalus was recorded as the direct successor to Caracalla. Elagabalus' mother and grandmother became senators and influenced the teenage Elagabalus throughout his reign.

He almost immediately married his first wife Julia Paula, divorced her a year later, then married a Vestal Virgin – Aquilia Severa. This created an uproar; traditionally, if a Vestal broke her vow, she was buried alive. His grandmother engineered the annulment of this marriage and married him to Annia Faustina (whose husband he'd just executed), but he went back to Severa, living with her unfaithfully until he died.

Referring to Elagabalus as a woman, Cassio Dio wrote about "her" falling in love with several men "she" married (or wanted to marry): his tutor Gannys – who helped overthrow Macrinus, a chariot driver named Hierocles (he was the husband and Elagabalus the wife), and an athlete named Zoticus.

Rome was also shocked when Elagabalus forced the worship of his Syrian god, Elagabal, as the chief deity of the Romans, over that of Jupiter. To increase his purity as a priest, he had himself circumcised and swore off pork – which utterly mystified the Romans, unfamiliar with Semitic customs. These behaviors alienated him from the Praetorian Guard – his protectors. His grandmother Maesa realized Elagabalus was too controversial to be taken seriously as emperor. No doubt someone would assassinate him eventually.

But it didn't have to mean the end of the Severan Dynasty. She had another grandson who might work out better – Severus Alexander, the 15-year-old son of her other daughter Julia Mamaea. She influenced Elagabalus to appoint his cousin Alexander as his heir, which he did – but then he suspected a coup d'état was in the works – which worried him because the Praetorian Guard liked Alexander better.

Elagabalus was right. On March 11, the Praetorian Guard attacked him and his mother, who was clinging tightly to him, killing them both and throwing their bodies into the Tiber. The Praetorian Guard then hailed Alexander as their new emperor on March 13, 222.

Alexander became emperor when his grandmother plotted the murder of her other grandson Elagabalus.
https://commons.wikimedia.org/wiki/File:Alexander_Severus_Musei_Capitolini_MC471_(cropped).jpg

Alexander ascended the throne at age 15 and reigned for 13 years as the last Severan emperor. He brought some stability to the empire but also confronted numerous, almost insurmountable challenges. He was admired by the Romans for his moderate, thoughtful, and dignified behavior – so different from his cousin Elagabalus.

He was a pious young man who prayed every morning in his private chapel – to the usual Roman deities, but also to Jesus, Abraham, and his ancestors – in a syncretistic mix reflecting his identity as a Roman along with his Middle Eastern heritage. Eusebius, Bishop of Caesarea in Palestine, wrote that he and his mother sat under the teaching of Origen – a well-known Christian scholar.

The peace and prosperity Rome had enjoyed in Alexander's first two years as emperor was threatened by the emergence of menacing challengers on the empire's eastern and northern borders. The ruthless and antagonistic Ardashir, the Persian founder of the Sassanid Dynasty, overthrew Parthia in 224 and invaded Roman provinces in Mesopotamia. Severus, accompanied by his mother, Julia Mamaea, led the Roman legions in a campaign against the Sassanians.

From Antioch, Alexander organized a three-pronged attack on the Sassanid Empire: his forces confronted Mesopotamia, while a second army marched through Armenia's mountains to invade Media, and a third army advanced on Babylon. The war ended inconclusively, with some embarrassing beatings by Ardashir's forces. Yet Alexander declared it a victory because Mesopotamia was retaken, and the Sassanid invasions stymied for a time.

Severus and Julia Mamaea then had to move their forces to the northern frontier – to the onslaught of Germanic tribes besieging Gaul and Raetia. Alarming hordes of Alemanni were crossing the Rhine and Danube. While traveling to confront the invaders, Severus and his mother were concerned about the breakdown in their army's discipline. When they were fighting the Sassanids, the Syrian legion had mutinied and declared a man named Taurinius their emperor. Alexander had crushed the revolt, and Taurinius drowned in the Euphrates. But could they trust their men now? Would they give up in the face of the Germans?

Unsure if they could defeat the invaders, Alexander and Julia paid a large bribe to induce the Germanic Alemanni to back down. This did not go over well with the military – they'd already received pay cuts and lapses in benefits. They thought Alexander was too docile and uninspiring as a leader. They sneered at him for following his mother's advice rather than listening to experienced generals and paying off the enemy rather than fighting them.

In 235, the northern legions rebelled, killing Alexander and his mother, and proclaiming Maximinus Thrax, a giant almost seven feet tall, as their new emperor. The assassination of Alexander, the last Syrian emperor, marked the close of the Severan Dynasty. The Crisis of the Third Century had begun. Without a clear candidate for emperor, the Roman Empire descended into a half-century of chaos, to the brink of collapse, faced with multiple contenders for the throne, increased invasions on the frontiers, civil wars, peasant revolts, plague, and economic disaster.

PART FOUR:
FINAL YEARS, SEPARATION, AND FALL
(AD 235-476)

Chapter 13: An Empire in Crisis

Chaos reigned for the next fifty years, from AD 235 to 284, as wars and internal chaos almost destroyed the empire in the Crisis of the Third Century. Peril loomed from without as barbarians continued to invade Roman territory. Multiple usurpers – 52 in all – competed for power; 26 claimants were approved as emperors by the Senate. A ghastly plague, the debasement of the currency, and economic depression were nearly Rome's undoing. Ultimately, Aurelian reunified the empire, and the ascension of Diocletian in 284 brought an end to the crisis.

Rome never had clear guidelines for who could be emperor, and this precipitated the Crisis of the Third Century. Traditionally, four factors came into play regarding the legitimacy of a new emperor: Senate confirmation, citizen's approval, military backing, and relationship to the previous emperor. The Severan Dynasty relied more on confirmation by the military than Senate approval, and several times after Nero's assassination, the military proclaimed a new emperor with no connection to the ruling dynasty and without asking the Senate first. However, if all four aspects backed a new emperor's ascension, he stood a better chance of staying on the throne.

Whenever an emperor died without a clear-cut heir, the empire usually descended into a chaotic situation, with various popular and powerful generals attempting to seize power, igniting civil wars. After Alexander's assassination, in powerplays that ravaged Rome, one general after another snatched power and proclaimed himself emperor.

In the pandemonium of the next five decades, Rome was led by a series of *barracks emperors*: men lacking political experience, aristocratic family lines, or any family connection to previous emperors. Barracks emperors got their power and backing from the barracks – the troops they led. They were warlords, relying on their successful experience as generals and the support of their legions.

This denarius, struck in 236, depicts Maximus Thrax, who was almost seven feet tall.

The exceptionally tall Maximus Thrax, declared the new emperor by the northern legions, was a prime example of a barracks emperor. His father was an accountant, probably from the Thracian tribe of eastern Europe. The Senate sniffed at his pedigree, but military men loved him for his legendary strength and skill as a soldier – and he certainly stood head and shoulders above anyone else.

Maximus never set foot in Rome during his three years as emperor. He immediately focused on defeating the Alemanni-Germanic tribes crossing the Rhine and infringing on Roman territory, establishing a temporary peace. The costs involved in his war campaigns and excessive soldiers' pay demanded high taxes, which irritated Rome's Senate and citizens.

When a revolt flared up in Africa in 238, the Senate threw their support behind the new usurpers: Gordian I and his son Gordian II. Maximus' problem was solved when Capelianus, governor of Numidia and archenemy of Gordian I, raided Carthage and killed Gordian II, after which Gordian I committed suicide. The senators feared Maximus' wrath because they'd supported his contenders; even so, they declared the grandson Gordian III as Caesar and two elderly patrician senators – Pupienus and Balbinus – as co-emperors.

Maximus marched on Rome to settle things, but his once-loyal troops, out of provisions and starving, were enraged at Maximus for executing his generals for what he considered cowardice in the unsuccessful siege of Aquileia. They mutinied, decapitating Maximus and his son, carrying their heads to Rome mounted on poles. Then the Praetorian Guard murdered Pupienus and Balbinus.

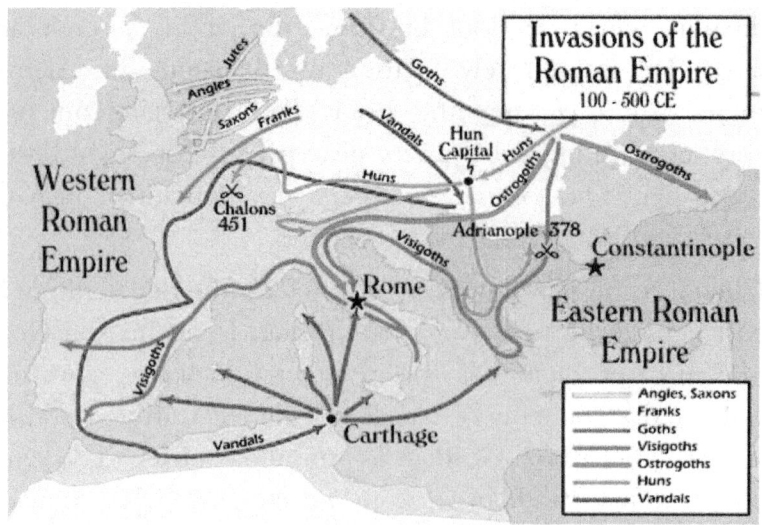

The incessant barbarian invasions contributed to the Roman Empire's ruin.

https://commons.wikimedia.org/wiki/File:Invasions_of_the_Roman_Empire_1.png

Once again, a power vacuum ensued, leading to multiple and successive uprisings of dozens of Roman generals – so fixated on power grabs they neglected defending the empire. The tribes surrounding the empire's frontiers exploited the exposed borders: the Carpians, Vandals, Goths, and Alamanni poured over the Danube and Rhine to raid Rome's northern provinces.

Philip the Arab, the former Praetorian Prefect, rose to the throne in 244 with Senate backing, bringing a measure of stability to the empire. During his five-year reign, Rome celebrated its millennium in 248 with three days of games in the Colosseum. According to Eusebius and Jerome, Philip – who grew up near Galilee – was the first Christian emperor, although coinage during his reign implied that he adhered to the polytheistic imperial religion. Even if not a Christian, he was sympathetic toward Christianity.

Because the new emperors were now mostly military men out on campaign somewhere, the center of government shifted away from Rome and to wherever the emperor was stationed with his troops –

usually somewhere in the eastern provinces. The Senate no longer held sway as the chief governmental body – it was now the equestrian class (cavalry) of the military rising to prominence.

Rome was not only cursed by invasions and inner turmoil, but from 249 to 262, the Plague of Cyprian swept the empire. From house to house, families would be infected, experiencing acute onset of symptoms including diarrhea, vomiting, fever, throat lesions, bleeding from the eyes, and tissue death in the arms and legs. Some experienced hearing loss, blindness, or loss of limbs. This was a new, terrifying plague – with symptoms never seen before – no one had acquired immunity. It killed the young adults and children as quickly as the older folks.

Cyprian, an African Berber and Bishop of Carthage, chronicled his first-hand observations of the horrific plague that bore his name. Bishop Cyprian preached to his flock to tend to the sick, as Jesus had commanded. The Christians provided care for those ravaged by the pandemic and buried the dead, heedless of their own danger.

https://commons.wikimedia.org/wiki/File:Cyprian_von_Karthago2.jpg

The pandemic began in Alexandria, Egypt, and spread to coastal centers throughout the empire, then moved inland. Physicians have analyzed the eyewitness account of Bishop Cyprian and other accounts to make educated guesses on what pathogen caused the deadly plague. Perhaps it was a hemorrhagic form of smallpox – but no one mentions the characteristic rash. More likely, it was a viral hemorrhagic fever – possibly a filovirus often transmitted from animals, such as monkeys or bats. Ebola is one example of a filovirus – it kills at least half of those infected – even with today's sophisticated medicine.

The plague severely weakened the empire – some cities lost over half their population. As the streets filled with the bodies of the dead, there was hardly anyone left to tend the farms – leading to famine. The military was also decimated – leaving the empire even more vulnerable to invasions.

Although the Germanic tribes in the north continued isolated attacks, the greatest threat to the empire was the Persian Sassanid Empire. Alexander had barely fended them off before his assassination, but now they were on the offensive again and had taken Antioch and Syria. After Valerian became emperor in 253, he headed east to confront the Sassanids, successfully recovering Antioch and Syria.

While fighting the Sassanid Empire, Valerian sent orders to the Senate ordering the empire-wide execution of Christian ministers and Christians who were Roman senators or equites (a wealthy political class) unless they worshipped the Roman gods. Lower-class citizens who refused to worship the Roman gods would be reduced to slavery. This indicated a shift toward the persecution of Christians by imperial decree but also revealed Christians had penetrated all classes of Roman society, including the Senate.

Among those executed were Pope Sixtus, Bishop Denis of Paris, Bishop Cyprian of Carthage, and Bishop Fructuosus of Tarragona, among countless others throughout the empire who were beheaded or burned at the stake. Two years after issuing this edict, the Sassanids captured Valerian, and he died in captivity. His son rescinded the anti-Christian orders.

And then it happened – the empire broke into pieces. Lacking a powerful central authority, the empire was divided into three competing empires. Gaul, Hispania, and Britain became the Gallic Empire in 260. Syria, Palestine, and Egypt broke off to become the Palmyrene Empire in 267. The central provinces remained under Rome's rule.

The three-way split rocked the Roman Empire to the core, already reeling from the incessant incursions of barbarian tribes and by ongoing internal unrest. Instead of building wealth by plundering other countries, they were now bleeding money to fund wars and losing soldiers faster than they could replace them. Rome increasingly relied on barbarian mercenaries known as foederati – tribes bound by treaty to support Rome.

Looting raids devastated the unprotected provinces. Barbarians continued streaming through the borders to settle in the empire; most were peacefully assimilated, but others came armed and ready to displace the existing populations. Eventually, the Illyrian emperors came to the rescue to stabilize the frontiers, beginning in 268. The Illyrians, from what is now the Balkans, had risen through Rome's military ranks to become commanders and eventually barracks emperors. They played an intrinsic part in recovering the provinces lost during the crisis and restoring a unified empire.

Claudius II Gothicus' stunning military defeat of the Goths helped end the Crisis of the Third Century.
https://commons.wikimedia.org/wiki/File:ClaudiusGothicusSC265569.jpg

One Illyrian emperor, Claudius II Gothicus, defeated a Gothic invasion into Macedonia and Greece in 268 – the turning point in the Crisis of the Third Century. He pushed the Alamanni back and recouped Hispania from the Gauls. Other resolute and zealous barracks emperors rehabilitated Rome's central authority. The pendulum was now swinging in the other direction.

But the damage had been done. Numerous once-flourishing cities of the western empire lay in ruins, their citizens dead or scattered. The economy was crushed. The Pax Romana was no more – now cities built thick, high walls for protection.

The Crisis of the Third Century included a financial catastrophe caused by multiple issues, including expensive military action, a corrupt and inefficient tax collection system, poor money management, bribing barbarians to stay away, and loss of manpower from the plague and warfare to work the farms, produce goods, and tend shops to sell them. For years, coinage devaluation persisted, leading to hyperinflation.

The Romans had a tradition that when a new emperor took the crown, he gave the soldiers a bonus. That money had to come from somewhere – especially when the country went through 26 emperors in 50 years. The emperors resorted to deflating the value of silver coins by adding in copper and bronze – rendering the silver denarius of no value – useless in trade and spawning rising prices.

The devalued coinage, unsafe travel, and sporadic pillaging by invading tribes profoundly disrupted the empire's vast trade network. The Pax Romana had collapsed, and merchants could no longer safely travel with agricultural and manufactured goods. The large plantations had no way to trade cash crops for manufactured goods, metals, wine, and grain. Commodities could no longer move freely from one end of the empire to the other. This led to economic decentralization. The Roman trade network never fully recovered.

Landowners changed their crops to ones that would sustain them and could be sold in local markets. Because they could no longer reliably import manufactured goods, they began local small-scale manufacturing, gradually becoming self-sufficient. The urban commoners transitioned to the safer rural areas with more food, giving up basic civil rights in exchange for protection. Urban regions throughout the empire slowly transitioned from sprawling metropolises to smaller walled cities defendable against raiding barbarians or opposing forces.

The transition of workers to rural areas produced the *coloni* – the beginnings of the medieval peasantry – half-free citizens that evolved into serfs in what would become a feudal society. In the western empire, the large landowners were becoming a law unto themselves, disregarding tax collectors and Rome's authority. Massive agricultural estates produced the only commodity of recognized value – food. The landholders rose in nobility status, while the merchant class shrank.

Some regions prospered through the chaotic Crisis of the Third Century – notably Egypt and Hispania – regions not especially affected by invading tribes and internal conflict. Trade flourished in these areas, and the people enjoyed a healthy economy. Because the eastern empire was more stable, Emperor Diocletian – who finally ended the Crisis of the Third Century – chose Nicomedia in Asia Minor as his seat of government, with Milan as the secondary governmental center. In the last days of the empire, the eastern section was far wealthier and more durable – able to survive when the western empire collapsed.

A crippling manpower shortage sprang from the plague and incessant warfare. Diocletian attempted to end the exodus from the cities by compelling workers to remain within their trades and forbidding workers and civil service workers to leave their jobs. Caught between economic collapse and authoritarian demands, the maltreated peasants banded together with escaped slaves, disillusioned civil officials, and military deserters in groups called *Bacaudae* or *Bagaudae* (from *fighters* in the Gallic language) – especially in Gaul and Hispania.

The mostly-peasant insurgents arose to defy imperial authority in the Crisis of the Third Century, persisting until the western empire collapsed. The Bacaudae attempted to counter the merciless exploitation of the coloni workers on the large manors and unjust laws against commoners and middle-class artisans and civil servants. Even some landowners rebelled against the crushing taxes, conscription of their workers for the military, and land garnishment by the state.

The Bacaudae revolts increased Rome's reliance on the barbarian foederati mercenaries – employing them to respond to the local unrest. Rome even settled the Iranian Alans tribe around Aurelianum (Orléans) in Gaul to subdue the Bacaudae. Although

Emperor Diocletian reinstituted order to the Roman Empire in the late third century, he appointed Maximian as his second-in-command to quash the Bacaudae. Maximian subdued them but never fully defeated them – in part because his army revolted, unwilling to fight the peasant rebels.

The Illyrian emperor Claudius II Gothicus, who had turned the tide of the crisis, died in the Plague of Cyprian in 270. The cavalry commander Aurelian rose to take his place as another Illyrian barracks emperor. Thought to be the son of a peasant farmer, he had proven himself in the military and, as emperor, achieved stunning victories in his five-year reign, restoring the broken Roman Empire.

The Aurelian Walls enclosed all the seven hills of Rome.
https://commons.wikimedia.org/wiki/File:Aurelian_Walls_-_Porta_Asinaria.jpg

Aurelian expelled the Vandals, Sarmatians, and Juthungi from northern Italia, defeated the Goths at the Danube, recovered the Palmyrene Empire from Queen Zenobia, restored the Gallic Empire to Rome, built massive ramparts encircling Rome that still stand today, and brought the three sections of the empire back into a unified whole by 274. Aurelian also reformed the coinage, which resulted in a rebellion of the mint workers, accustomed to stealing the silver. He enhanced the free-food distribution to the poor, giving bread, salt, olive oil, and pork.

Seizing the opportunity to vanquish the Sassanid Empire, which was experiencing a leadership crisis, Aurelian embarked on a new campaign in 275. However, he was murdered on his way east by Praetorian Guard officers who erroneously thought they had been marked for execution. His wife, Ulpia Severina, continued his reign in the eight-month interval while the military and Senate were trying to decide what to do next.

Remorseful over their popular emperor's murder, the army handed the right to choose his successor back to the Senate. The Senate was hesitant –, they hadn't elected an emperor in decades – after this election, they never would again. Finally, they proclaimed the elderly Marcus Claudius Tacitus as the new emperor, with the army's polite sanction.

Tacitus restored the Senate to the powers they held in the old days, then turned his attention to the Foederati mercenaries supplementing Aurelian's forces. Once Aurelian was dead - and the Sassanid campaign canceled - they were stranded in the eastern provinces and started plundering towns. Tacitus subdued the tribal mercenaries, gaining the title Gothicus Maximus, then died of a fever on his way back west. His half-brother Florian, the Praetorian Prefect, became the next emperor for three months until he was assassinated by his army.

Florian was succeeded by Probus, another Illyrian barracks emperor who had distinguished himself in the military and had been appointed Supreme Chief of the eastern provinces by Tacitus. In his six-year reign, he continued his successful military campaigns, said to have fought in every front in the empire during his lifetime. By protecting the frontiers, the empire once again experienced stability and prosperity. Whenever there was a lull in fighting, Probus put his soldiers to useful tasks, such as draining marshes or replanting vineyards – further enhancing the economy. Some of the military men were disgruntled with these orders and assassinated Probus, proclaiming Marcus Aurelius Carus, commander of the Praetorian Guard, as their new emperor.

Before he was struck by lightning – ending his nine-month reign – Carus suppressed the Senate's authority for good. His sons Carinus and Numerian succeeded him as co-emperors until Numerian's soldiers smelled a putrid odor coming from his covered litter while marching home from Persia and discovered he was dead. The commander of his bodyguard, Diocletian, declared Numerian's father-in-law Aper had murdered Numerian and ran his sword through Aper. The military hailed Diocletian as their new emperor, but Carinus (rumored to have married nine wives) was still co-emperor. Heading east from Rome and confronting Diocletian, Carinus died in the struggle.

Diocletian ended the Crisis of the Third Century as the new emperor of Rome, but systemic difficulties remained. The issue of succession had still not been settled, leaving the door open for more civil wars. The empire's stupendous size – stretching across three continents – made it impossible for one man to tackle multiple invasions or other challenges simultaneously. Although Diocletian rescued the empire from total collapse, its foundations were weakened, and the beginning of the end loomed ahead.

Chapter 14: Diocletian and Constantine the Great

Two eminent emperors - Diocletian and Constantine the Great - dominated the next five decades, from 284 to 337, bringing momentous changes to the Roman Empire. Diocletian was distinctive for dividing the empire into four parts, persecuting Christians on the greatest scale ever, and being the first emperor to abdicate his throne. Constantine was renowned for transitioning the empire's capital from Rome to Byzantium, protecting Christians and all religions with the Edict of Milan, convening the Nicaean Council to sort out Christian theology, and receiving Christian baptism on his deathbed.

Diocletian instituted reforms to further stabilize the empire and address systemic issues, transforming ideological, administrative, legal, military, and economic affairs. His ideological reforms involved a strong central authority imposing imperial values on the provinces, using revisionist history. Imperial propaganda characterized the empire's history from Augustus until the tetrarchy as incessant internal conflict, tyrannical totalitarianism, and disintegrated government - all now repaired by Diocletian, "founder of eternal peace."

Administrative reforms supported an autocracy, dismissing a cooperative government between the emperor, Senate, and military. Everything was now run from the top down, with everyone answering ultimately to Diocletian. He reduced the Praetorian Guard to a defensive garrison for Rome – it would no longer choose emperors and assassinate them.

Diocletian ended the Crisis of the Third Century and masterminded the Tetrarchy.
https://commons.wikimedia.org/wiki/File:Diocletian_Bueste.JPG

In legal affairs, Diocletian's government published law books on precedent and law codes. Governors were now called judges (*iudex*), and the entire empire had a right of appeal. Diocletian was the last emperor to follow classic Roman law; his successors followed eastern and Greek legal philosophy.

Diocletian beefed up the size of his troops – boasting that the four tetrarchs each had more soldiers than previous emperors had for the whole empire. He stationed his men on the frontiers, keeping the borders secure. More soldiers meant more people to pay, meaning higher taxes.

Diocletian's new tax system was tied to an annual census of the entire population and how much land was owned. Tax day was September 1. He instituted a new system of coinage, with five coins: gold, silver, copper-silver, and two copper-only coins of two sizes. Their value didn't reflect the intrinsic worth of the metal, so inflation reared its head, causing Diocletian to order a price freeze.

Realizing the impossibility of one person maintaining the stability of the gigantic empire, Diocletian appointed Maximian, a stellar general, as Caesar and his co-ruler. Diocletian gave primary attention to the eastern part of the empire, and Maximian dealt with subduing the irksome Bagaudae in the west. In 293, Diocletian further organized the empire into a *tetrarchy (rule of four)* with two lead emperors called *Augusti* – Diocletian and Maximian – and two junior emperors – the *Caesares*, who answered to the Augusti and would succeed them. The two Caesares were Galerius and Constantius, who were adopted by Diocletian and Maximian.

Maximian's son (Maxentius) and Constantius' son (Constantine) were groomed in Diocletian's court to step into the Caesares (junior emperor) positions whenever Diocletian or Maximian died, and Galerius or Constantius moved to the top emperor positions. With this system, Diocletian hoped to install a fixed system of succession and avoid all the usurpers and civil wars. Strategically, four co-rulers could be positioned in four points of the empire to resist invaders and sustain smooth internal affairs.

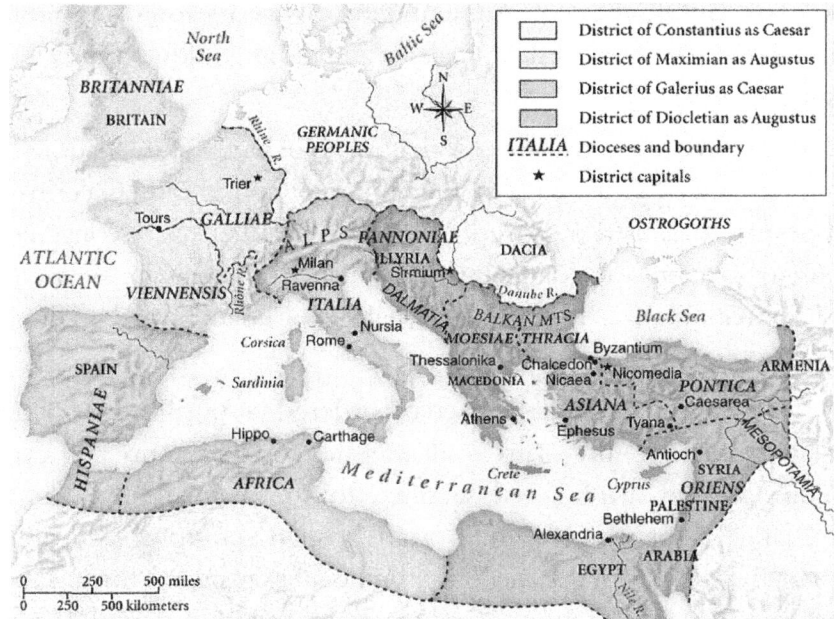

The Tetrarchy divided the Roman Empire into four sections ruled by Diocletian, Maximian, Galerius, and Constantius.
https://commons.wikimedia.org/wiki/File:Tetrarchy_map3.jpg

Rome was no longer the capital of the empire – now, the four co-rulers were stationed in four capitals. Diocletian's capital was Nicomedia (in modern-day Turkey), defending against the Persian Sassanids and the Balkans. Galerius' capital was Sirmium (modern Serbia), close to the Danube river – the homeland of the Illyrian emperors. Maximum was stationed in Milan in northern Italy – guarding against invasions from over the Alps. He was the administrator for Italy and the African provinces. Constantius was stationed in Augusta Treverorum (Germany), near the Rhine, and he kept affairs in western Europe running smoothly.

Following a successful war against the Sassanids, in which Galerius captured King Narseh's harem, children, and treasury, the king was eager to sign the Peace of Nisibis to get his wives and children back. Flushed with victory, Diocletian and Galerius returned to Antioch, where they offered sacrifices of thanksgiving to the gods. But there was a problem – the divinators couldn't read the entrails of the sacrificed animals – and thus couldn't predict the future.

Why were the gods silent? What was blocking the divinations? It must be those Christians in the imperial household. Galerius, a passionate pagan who viewed a purge of Christians as a convenient way to get rid of political rivals, pushed Diocletian to violent extermination of Christians, although Diocletian hoped to do so without bloodshed.

At Galerius' urging, Diocletian ordered a purification of the palace and the entire army – all members of the court and every soldier in the army must sacrifice to the Roman gods or be discharged – or worse. When one Christian centurion, Marcellus, heard that he had no choice, he immediately resigned his position, throwing his belt, sword, and insignia to the ground, loudly proclaiming he would only obey Jesus Christ the eternal King. He was arrested on the spot and beheaded. Diocletian's Christian butler Peter was boiled alive.

Thus began the Great Persecution of Christians, who made up about ten percent of the population. Galerius and Diocletian issued edicts purging Christians in the government and military, razing churches, burning Bibles, forbidding Christians to assemble, imprisoning all bishops and priests, and punishing everyone refusing to sacrifice to the Roman deities. The deacon Romanus of Palestine had his tongue cut off and was later executed. An entire congregation in Phrygia was burned alive. Young men were castrated, and virgin girls were sent to brothels. In Africa and the Middle East, Maximinus had Christians blinded in one eye and sent to work in the mines.

Constantius only halfheartedly enforced the edicts at his end of the empire: he mostly only worshiped one god – Sol Invictus, the sun god – and was sympathetic to Christian monotheists. Christians in Gaul and Britain largely escaped the atrocities of Galerius, Maximinus, and Diocletian. Even most pagans throughout the empire were unwilling to support the persecution.

In Armenia, a client-state of Rome, King Tiridates of Armenia had thrown his Christian secretary Gregory into a pit for refusing to worship a goddess with him. Thirteen years later (now in Diocletian's day), King Tiridates fell prey to mental illness, wandering through the forests like a wild boar. His sister had a dream that Gregory could cure him. They hauled the emaciated Gregory up from underground, and he prayed for King Tiridates. The king was healed and converted to Christianity, declaring it the official religion of Armenia in 301. Armenia became the first Christian state, right in the middle of the Great Persecution.

Eventually, Galerius rescinded the edicts against Christianity in 311, passing the Edict of Toleration – stating persecution had done nothing to convert Christians to the Roman gods. Quite the reverse – the Christians' resolve to remain true to their faith had precipitated great admiration, impelling more converts to Christianity. In the words of Tertullian, "The blood of the martyrs was the seed of the church."

Diocletian fell ill in 304, collapsing soon after the grand opening of a circus just next to his palace. Throughout the winter, he remained confined inside, sparking rumors he had died. Finally, on March 1, 305, he appeared in public again, ghastly thin. Galerius quickly snatched the opportunity of Diocletian's illness to rearrange the tetrarch to his advantage. In Diocletian's original plan, Galerius would succeed Diocletian, and Constantius would replace Maximian, then Constantine and Maxentius would become the Caesars. Galerius bullied the weakened Diocletian into putting Constantine and Maxentius to the side and choosing Severus

(Galerius' drinking buddy and a senior army official) and Maximinus (Galerius' nephew) as the new Caesars.

Gravely ill, Diocletian abdicated in 305 – a first for Roman emperors – and his co-emperor Maximian retired with him. As planned, Galerius and Constantius moved up to become the top emperors, and as unplanned by Diocletian, Severus and Maximinus became the two junior emperors. Diocletian lived four more years, watching his carefully planned tetrarchy fall to pieces.

Constantine had been living in Diocletian's palace for the past 12 years, receiving a formal education to prepare him to become the next Caesar. Now, his destiny had abruptly changed. Diocletian had retired to Dalmatia, Galerius was the new emperor living in the palace, and it was not a safe place for Constantine – who represented a threat to Galerius's ambitions.

Constantine's father – Constantius, Galerius' co-emperor now – came to the rescue, recalling his son from Nicomedia to help his campaign in Britain. Constantine got Galerius drunk, and he granted Constantine leave to go to Britain; Constantine fled during the night, charging down the road on his horse before Galerius sobered up and changed his mind. For the next year, Constantius and Constantine campaigned in Britain, fighting the blue-tattooed Picts beyond Hadrian's Wall.

Constantius succumbed to a prolonged illness – probably leukemia – in July 306; before he died, he declared his wish for Constantine to become Augustus in his place (as was Diocletian's intent but overturned by Galerius). King Chrocus, a Foederati from the Germanic Alamanni, proclaimed Constantine as Augustus – the new co-emperor. Constantius' troops backed Constantine; Gaul and Britain welcomed his rule, but Hispania spurned it.

Constantine the Great enacted the Edit of Milan, granting safety and freedom of religion for Christians and all religions.

Constantine sent a dispatch to Galerius, informing him of his father's death, explaining that his army had forced upon him the rank of Augustus in his father's place. He apologized for the irregularity but asked Galerius to recognize his natural claim as his father's successor.

Galerius was enraged – threatening to set both the letter and Constantine on fire. His counselors advised him to take a middle path to avoid outright war – neither rejecting Constantine's claims nor accepting them. Rather, he should grant Constantine the rank of Caesar, replacing Severus, who would move up to Augustus. Both Galerius and Constantine agreed to this compromise, making Constantine ruler of Gaul, Britain, and Hispania.

Although not yet a Christian, Constantine decreed an end to the persecution of Christians in his section of the empire. His ascension to Caesar made Maxentius – Maximian's son – jealous. Like Constantine, Maxentius had been trained under Diocletian to become Caesar. Now Maximinus had usurped Maxentius' spot, due to Galerius' manipulation of Diocletian. So, Maxentius declared himself emperor in Italy.

Just to review – we now have three men named Max to keep straight: Maximian – the retired Augustus, Maxentius – his son, and Maximinus – Galerius' nephew and the current Caesar.

Galerius sent Severus to deal with Maxentius – but Severus' army had previously been Maximian's – and they defected to their former commander's son. Severus was imprisoned and later executed. Maximian came out of retirement to become Maxentius' co-emperor, offering his daughter Fausta in marriage to Constantine and promising to help him ascend to emperor if he would help them against Galerius. Constantine gave verbal support to father and son but never sent troops to help. Then Maximian and Maxentius fell out.

Now, Diocletian also came out of retirement briefly in 308 for a conference with Galerius and Maximian. Their joint decision made Galerius' old friend Licinius the Augustus (emperor) in the west, with Constantine as his Caesar. Galerius would still be Augustus in the east, with Maximinus continuing as his Caesar. Maximian and Diocletian would go back into retirement. This made Maxentius a nobody – a usurper. No sooner had that been decided than Maximinus declared himself Augustus, and Constantine refused to be demoted back to Caesar. Maximian committed suicide in 310, and Galerius died in 311.

Now we're down to two men named Max: Maximinus – Galerius' nephew and Maxentius – Maximian's son, both self-proclaimed – but mostly unrecognized – emperors.

The tetrarchy was in tatters – the contenders at this point were Licinius, Constantine, Maxentius, and Maximinus. Constantine allied with Licinius, and Maxentius allied with Maximinus. In 312, Constantine crossed the Alps into Italy. After defeating two cities, the rest of Italy welcomed him with open arms. Surrounded by the

Aurelian Walls, defended by the Praetorian Guard, and with an army twice the size of Constantine's, Maxentius felt safe in Rome.

After his vision, Constantine went to battle with the labarum – the first two letters of the Greek word for Christ – on his helmet, his soldiers' shields, and his banners.

https://commons.wikimedia.org/wiki/File:Schlosskirche_(Blieskastel)_Chi-Rho.jpg

Then, Constantine had a vision while marching in the heat of the day. Above the sun, he saw a cross of light with the inscription, "*In Hoc Signo Vinces*" ("In this sign, you shall conquer"). He had a dream that night where Jesus repeated the same message. Still a pagan at this point (but growing less so by the minute), Constantine had insignia made with the *labarum* – an X (Chi) over a P (Rho) – the first two letters in the Greek word ΧΡΙΣΤΟΣ (Christos). He wore a helmet adorned with the Chi Rho, and his soldiers marched into battle with the labarum of Christ on their standards and shields.

Constantine and Maxentius faced off at the Tiber. After a brief battle, Constantine forced Maxentius' cavalry and infantry back, some falling into the river and drowning, Maxentius among them. Constantine marched into Rome, received with rejoicing. He chose not to offer the usual sacrifices to Jupiter but did meet with the Senate, promising them a return to their former status in his new government. The Senate declared him "greatest Augustus."

In 313, Constantine headed to Milan for the wedding of his half-sister Constantia to his ally Licinius. While there, the two emperors agreed on the Edict of Milan, which granted legal status to Christians and protection from persecution. It mandated freedom of worship to Christians and other religions: "that each one may have the free opportunity to worship as he pleases." The Edict directed that buildings used for Christian meeting places be restored to the Christians. Christians were to be released from prisons and forced labor in the mines.

Was Constantine still a pagan? Licinius was, but Constantine likely was not – for one thing, he didn't worship the gods in Rome in the previous year, although his coinage showed Sol Invictus – the sun god – for several more years. Eusebius said that after his vision, Constantine sought some Christian teachers to help him understand what was going on. They told him that Jesus was the only son of the one and only God and that the sign of the cross he saw in the sky was a symbol of immortality – Jesus' victory over death. Constantine devoted himself to reading the Bible, making Christian priests his advisors, and honoring Jesus with his devotion. He did not get baptized (yet), but he invited Christian ministers to spend time with him, eat with him, and travel with him. He donated copious amounts to church building projects.

When Diocletian was emperor, he chose Nicomedia as his capital, strategically located in western Turkey between the Aegean and the Black Sea – where Europe and Asia meet, easily accessible by sea to Africa and the Middle East. Constantine wanted to build a new capital in the same region that would represent the unification of the east with the west, serving as a center of culture, learning, and trade. He chose Byzantium, a Greek city close to Nicomedia but right on the Strait of Istanbul. In 324, he enlarged and rebuilt

Byzantium – now known as "New Rome" or Constantinople. It became the most affluent city in Europe; within two centuries, its population would grow to an estimated one million – the largest city in the world at that time.

Constantine convened the Council of Nicaea to unite Christians on basic theology. https://commons.wikimedia.org/wiki/File:Nicea.jpg

In 325, several hundred Christian deacons and bishops gathered in Nicaea – near to where Constantinople was being built. An open copy of the Gospels lay on the conference table. Constantine entered the hall in his royal robes, briefly greeting the Christian leaders and advising them of the purpose of the meeting: to agree on some divisive issues. "Division in the church is worse than war," he said.

The bishops and deacons had met to debate the doctrine of the Holy Trinity. Arius, a priest in Alexandria, thought Jesus wasn't equal with God because he was born as a human – thus having a beginning, while God was infinite, with no beginning or end. The churchmen compared Arius' teaching to the Gospel of John, which begins by stating that the *Logos* – Jesus – was in the beginning with God, and through him, all things were made. Thus, even though Jesus's physical body had a beginning, he existed as part of the

Godhead from infinity. From their discussion, the council determined that the Father, Son, and Holy Spirit were equal members of the Trinity. They banished the Arian leaders for heresy and established the *Nicene Creed* – a statement of the basic doctrines of Christianity.

Just after the Feast of Easter in 337, Constantine became critically ill. Realizing death was near, he called the bishops, telling them he'd hoped to be baptized in the Jordan River, where Jesus was baptized, but he now understood he needed to be baptized immediately. The historian Eusebius of Caesarea wrote that Bishop Eusebius of Nicomedia baptized Constantine into the Christian faith. The emperor died shortly after on May 22, 337.

The reigns of Diocletian and Constantinople guided Rome through its greatest persecution of Christianity, followed by freedom of religion for all faiths, with an emperor who actively promoted Christianity. The long reigns of both men brought stability to the empire. Although Diocletian's tetrarchy failed, it was an ingenious plan to provide administrative centers in four points of the far-flung empire and an organized means of succession. Constantine replaced the tetrarchy with dynastic succession; however, he followed Diocletian's concept of multiple rulers by designating his three sons as co-rulers after his death.

Chapter 15: The Constantinian Dynasty and the Fall of the West

Constantine had intended the running of the empire to be a family affair after his death, with his three sons - Constantine II, Constantius II, and Constans - as the emperors, and their cousins - Dalmatius and Hannibalianus - as the Caesars. The empire was meant to be divided five ways, with each emperor or Caesar ruling a section. Constantine's arrangement only lasted weeks, as his three sons slaughtered Dalmatius and Hannibalianus, along with two uncles and three other cousins.

The three brothers then divided the empire three ways. The oldest - Constantine - took Britain, Gaul, and Hispania, but as guardian of his youngest brother Constans - not yet of age - Constantine also oversaw Italy, Africa, and Illyricum. Constantius received the Asian provinces, Egypt, Greece, and Thrace.

Constantine II resented sharing power with his younger brothers. When Constans came of age, Constantine refused to relinquish Italy, Africa, and Illyricum. In the ensuing battle, Constantine II was killed in AD 340, leaving Constans with the entire western empire and most of northern Africa to rule – in uneasy peace with Constantius II, ruler of the eastern empire. Ten years later, Constans' inept leadership cost him the support of his troops, who defected to the usurper Magnentius and killed Constans in 350. Three years later, Magnentius faced off against Constantius II. After spending the day praying in a nearby church, Constantius defeated Magnentius, becoming sole emperor of the entire Roman Empire.

Constantius II, son of Constantine the Great, ruled with his brothers and then on his own for 24 years.
https://commons.wikimedia.org/wiki/File:07_constantius2Chrono354.png

The three sons of Constantine the Great were, nominally at least, Christians – although they overlooked the "love your brother as yourself" part. Constans supported the stance of the First Nicaean Council regarding the Trinity. Constantius did not agree with the Nicene Creed, but he didn't agree with Arius either – he followed

Semi-Arianism. Most Christians in the empire had no clue what the controversy was all about.

At the urgent request of Pope Julius, Constans and Constantius convened the Council of Serdica in 343 to resolve the theological conflict. Instead, it accentuated the tensions between the theological camps, causing a greater divide, with the eastern churches leaning toward Arianism, and the western European churches supporting the Nicene Creed. The two emperors agreed that each would support their preferred clergy and theology in their ends of the empire.

Throughout his reign, Constantius clashed with the Sassanid Empire in the Perso-Roman wars, in which King Shapur II usually prevailed but never achieved a conclusive triumph. Shapur attacked Nisibis (on the border of what is now Turkey and Syria) in 350, with an incredible strategy. He broke the dams on the Mygdonius River, flooding the valley, then sailed his fleet right up to the city's ramparts, collapsing a section of the wall. His plan went awry when his war elephants got bogged down in the mud, and he had to retreat. Overnight, the industrious Nisibis forces repaired the breach; then, Shapur got word that the Huns were invading Persia, so he had to abandon Nisibis to defend his lands.

Supported by the local tribes, Shapur invaded Roman Mesopotamia in 359. With 100,000 men, he encircled Amida (in Asian Turkey) where six Roman legions waited. Although the legions fought fiercely, and the Roman Scorpion siege engines decimated the Sassanids, Shapur eventually breached the walls. He sacked the city, killing most of the Roman officers and deporting the population to Persia. It was a Pyrrhic victory – Shapur lost one-third of his army, and his tribal allies deserted him.

After Constans died, Constantius discovered that single-handedly running an empire stretching across three continents was overwhelming. His brothers were dead – who would help him? His cousin Julian was only six when Constantius and his brothers were killing off most of their male relatives, and now Julian was a young man. In 354, Constantius appointed Julian to rule Gaul, which he did so superbly that his soldiers declared him emperor in 360. Constantius was too busy fighting the Persians to do anything about Julian.

Finally, during a lull in the hostilities with the Sassanids, Constantius marched west with his armies to confront Julian but fell deathly ill with a fever on the way. He asked Bishop Euzoius to baptize him, then died in November 361, declaring Julius as his successor.

Julian was raised Christian but converted to paganism around age 20, initiated into the secret Eleusinian Mysteries for the cult of Demeter and Persephone. He was eager to revive the ancient Greco-Roman polytheistic religion while subduing Christianity. Julian's religious reforms targeted affluent, upper-class Christians; he didn't mind if the commoners were Christians, but he wanted the ruling classes to follow the traditional pagan ways. He did not promote the violent persecution of Diocletian's day, knowing it had backfired and strengthened the church. He preferred softer measures, such as removing state stipends for bishops and reversing privileges and favors Christians had enjoyed.

His biggest obstacle – one he complained about bitterly – was Christian charity. Julian wrote to the pagan priest Arsacius, "It is disgraceful that, when no Jew ever has to beg, and the impious Galileans [Christians] support not only their own poor but ours as well, all men see that our people lack aid from us."

Although Rome had a state-funded food dole for the poor, the concept of personal charity – individuals helping those who couldn't return the favor – was foreign to Greco-Roman polytheists. In stark contrast, Jesus taught his followers to throw banquets and invite the poor, the crippled, the lame, and the blind (Luke 14:12-14). And that's what the pagan world observed: Christians caring for the poor, the orphans, the widows, and the sick – even burying the dead during the plagues.

At any rate, Julian did not have long to overturn Christianity and reinvigorate paganism. His reign lasted less than two years. Despite peace offers from the Sassanids, he wanted to gain fame and glory by trouncing the Persians once and for all, which didn't go well. In the Battle of Samarra, a spear pierced his gut, and he died three days later in 363.

The day after Julian died, the Roman military elected their commander Jovian as emperor. Although he lived only eight months, he restored Christianity to favored status in the empire. He died in mysterious circumstances, found dead in his tent while traveling to Constantinople – perhaps from poisonous fumes.

Valentinian ruled the western Roman Empire beginning in 364. By Classical Numismatic Group, Inc. *https://www.cngcoins.com/*, CC BY-SA 2.5, https://commons.wikimedia.org/w/index.php?curid=93817299

The military and civil officials met in Nicaea, finally choosing Valentinian, a tribune who had served under Constantius and Julian. Valentinian was crowned emperor in February 364, then appointed his brother Valens to be his co-ruler. Valens made Constantinople his capital, while Valentinian ruled from Milan in northern Italy.

Two simultaneous challenges confronted Valentinian on November 1, 365: the Germanic Alamanni were invading Gaul, and Procopius - the last descendent of the Constantinian Dynasty - had revolted. His first instinct was to head east to help Valens, but the cities in Gaul urgently begged him to come. After a year of battles and initial defeats, he forced the Alamanni out of Gaul. Meanwhile, Valens captured Procopius and executed him by having him torn apart.

When a crisis in Britain distracted Valentinian, the Alamanni crept back across the Rhine, raiding and plundering. This time, Valentinian conspired to have Vithicabius - a key Alamanni chieftain - assassinated by his bodyguard. Valentinian then mustered a gigantic force to cross the Rhine and invade the Alamanni lands in southwestern Germany, determined to permanently overcome them. While on a reconnaissance mission, Valentinian was almost captured by an enemy ambush. The Romans defeated the Alamanni mountaintop encampment in the fierce Battle of Solicinium, but with heavy casualties. Valentinian then ordered a series of fortresses built along the Rhine to keep the Alamanni on their side of the river.

The crisis in Britain that had distracted Valentinian was the Great Conspiracy. The Roman garrison guarding Hadrian's Wall had defected, letting the fierce Picts into Britain. Meanwhile, a joint force of Scots, Saxons, and Attacotti (possibly from Ireland) invaded by sea. Simultaneously, Franks and Saxons attacked northern Gaul. Nearly all the Roman settlements of northern and western Britain were overcome: the tribes sacked their cities, murdering, raping, and enslaving the population.

The Roman response was initially unsuccessful, but finally, the commander Flavius Theodosius with his son Theodosius I (who later became emperor) crossed the channel and marched to Londinium (London). Using stealth and ambush, his forces attacked the raiding tribes, recouping the captured people and livestock. His forces chased the barbarians back to their homelands, retook Hadrian's Wall, and regarrisoned the abandoned forts.

In 373, war broke out on the Danube with the Germanic Quadi and their Iranian-Sarmatian allies, who had been steadily migrating west. Tension flared over Valentinian building forts in Quadi territory. Marcellinus, in charge of the building project, held a banquet for the Quadi and Sarmatians, under the pretense of initiating peace negotiations, but then he killed the Quadi king Gabinius. The enraged Quadi and Sarmatians charged across the Danube, ravaging the region of Valeria.

Valentinian marched to Carnuntum (in what is now southern Austria), where the apprehensive Sarmatians sent ambassadors seeking forgiveness for participating in the fray. Overlooking Marcellianus' treachery and determined to make an example of the Quadi, Valentinian crossed the Danube, pillaging their lands.

In November 374, a Quadi deputation arrived at Valentinian's camp. They complained about Roman fortresses being built on their land and explained that not all the Quadi chiefs had entered peace treaties with Rome – it was the hold-outs who were attacking. Valentinian exploded in a rage, screaming at the envoys, when he suddenly had a stroke and dropped dead. As founder of the Valentinian Dynasty, his sons Gratian and Valentinian II succeeded him as rulers of the western empire, while his brother Valens continued to rule the eastern empire from Constantinople.

The Aqueduct of Valens in Constantinople (now Istanbul) was completed in 373. https://commons.wikimedia.org/wiki/File:Valens_2012_DK.jpg

While Valentinian had been contending with the Alamanni, Quadi, and Sarmatians, Valens was campaigning against the Goths, the Persians, and the Saracens. A bungled attempt to resettle the Goths (displaced by the Huns) in the Balkans led to the Gothic War of 376-377. Valens' forces unsuccessfully collided with the Goths for two years. Jealous of the western emperor Gratian's recent victory over the Alamanni, Valens took over the campaign against the Goths himself – not a great plan, given his mediocrity in military affairs. As 10,000 Goths were marching on Adrianople (in Thrace), Gratian sent a message that his troops were on the way to assist Valens, urging Valens to wait for them before engaging the Goths. The headstrong Valens, not wanting to share the glory, proceeded anyway.

The battle was one of the worst defeats in Roman history. Some overeager Roman forces attacked without orders, leaving the lines in disarray. The Gothic cavalry returned from a raiding mission just in time, surrounding the Roman troops and decimating their numbers. Abandoned on the field, Valens was presumably killed, although his body was never found. At least two-thirds of Rome's eastern forces were destroyed, including most of the experienced generals.

After Valens' death, Gratian appointed Theodosius I as the next co-emperor. He was the son of the hero Flavius Theodosius, who vanquished Britain's Great Conspiracy. Theodosius negotiated peace with the Goths by permitting them to settle in Roman territory but maintaining their military and political autonomy – and serving as mercenaries in Rome's imperial forces.

In 383, the usurper Magnus Maximus proclaimed himself emperor, invaded Gaul, killed Emperor Gratian, and assumed rule over Gaul, Britain, and Hispania. Theodosius counterattacked in 388, defeating Maximus, executing him, and restoring his younger half-brother Valentinian II as emperor of the west.

When Theodosius I died in 396, his throne went to his two sons: Honorius was to rule in the West and Arcadius in the East – but both boys were still under ten years old. Honorius was dominated by his uncle, Stilicho the Vandal, and Arcadius' Praetor Prefect Rufinus controlled the eastern empire. Instead of cooperating, Stilicho and Rufinus undermined each other's military efforts, weakening the already stressed empire. Even when Honorius and Arcadius came of age, they remained puppet emperors.

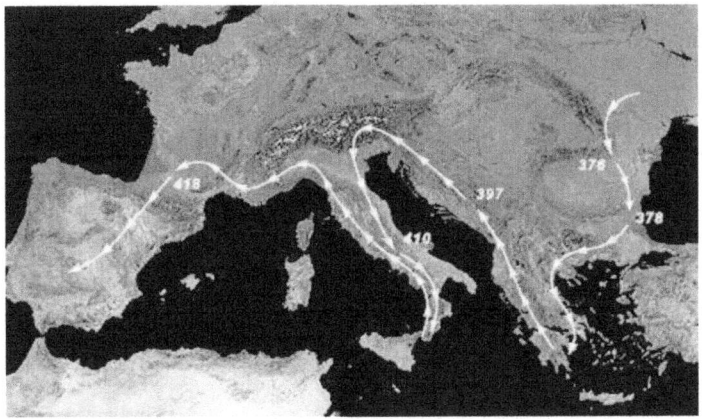

The Visigoths spoke a Germanic language and probably originated in Scandinavia, then migrated north of the Black Sea. This map shows their migration south and west in the last days of the Roman Empire. https://commons.wikimedia.org/wiki/File:Visigoth_migrations.jpg

Stilicho had several run-ins with Alaric – a Visigoth who'd once served as a mercenary under Theodosius I but had gone rogue, becoming King of the Visigoths (western Goths). Sometimes Alaric was fighting Stilicho, and other times Stilicho was plotting to take over the eastern empire with Alaric's help. Alaric invaded Italy during a famine in 410, raiding the countryside to feed his army of Goths and runaway slaves. He contacted Honorius, offering to leave Italy in exchange for food, but Honorius refused.

The famine was so dreadful that Jerome reported cannibalism going on in the city of Rome. Alaric easily took Rome and sacked it – the starving people were helpless. His men stole anything of value they could carry away and ransacked and burned the important buildings around the Senate House and Forum, but mostly spared the basilicas of Peter and Paul. The Goths captured many Romans, ransoming some, selling some as slaves, and raping and killing others. Rome had not been sacked in nearly eight centuries – the eternal city was increasingly vulnerable and frail.

Alaric and the Visigoths ravaged southern Italy, but their plan to cross to Africa failed when a storm destroyed their ships. A few months after sacking Rome, Alaric fell ill and died in Italy. His band headed to southwestern Gaul, establishing the Visigoth Kingdom, which helped the western empire fight Attila the Hun four decades later.

While Rome was being sacked in 410, Britain was falling apart, as the remaining Roman troops proclaimed a series of usurpers. The last – Constantine III – raided Gaul and defeated Honorius' army. When the Roman citizens in Britain asked Honorius to help them evict Constantine, he told them they were on their own. Rome had essentially abandoned Britain.

Arcadius' only son Theodosius II became co-Augustus with his father while still an infant – the youngest Roman emperor. When Arcadius died in 408, Theodosius became emperor of the eastern empire at age seven. His Praetorian Prefect, Anthemius, managed governmental affairs at first, then in 414, Theodosius' older sister Pulcheria was pronounced Augustus, ruling until Theodosius came of age.

The Huns threatened Constantinople while Theodosius was campaigning in Persia. Theodosius returned to Constantinople in 424 and paid the Huns 350 pounds of gold to live peacefully in the empire. Nine years later, when Attila the Hun rose to dominance, he doubled the annual payment to 700 pounds. In 423, the western emperor Honorius died, and Theodosius killed the usurper Joannes and installed his six-year-old cousin Valentinian III as emperor of the western empire, with the boy's mother, Galla Placidia, as regent.

The western Roman Empire was crumbling around the edges. Britain was gone, part of Africa was gone, Hispania was slipping away, and Gaul was held by the Visigoths in the southwest and the Franks in the northeast. In 428, 80,000 Alans and Vandals, united under King Genseric, crossed the Straits of Gibraltar to Mauritania in Africa, then spread to Numidia, kicking out the Roman ruler Boniface.

In 439, the Vandals captured Carthage. Their powerful navy controlled the area, crushing the western empire's economy, dependent on Africa for tax revenues and grain. Both emperors sent troops to launch an attack from Sicily. But Attila the Hun and the Persians took this opportunity to attack on two fronts, so the forces in Sicily were recalled. After a catastrophic loss to the Huns, the Romans' annual tribute tripled to 2100 pounds of god.

Theodosius II fell from a horse and died in 450, with no sons and no chosen successor. After a month of discussions (but *not* consulting the western emperor Valentinian III), Theodosius' personal assistant Marcian was chosen as the next emperor of the eastern empire. The lack of input from Valentinian III indicates how politically separate the eastern and western sections of the empire had become by AD 450. The relationship between east and west at this point was more like two large countries in friendly alliance rather than two sections of the same empire.

Atilla the Hun was one of the most feared barbarians who menaced the Roman Empire.

https://upload.wikimedia.org/wikipedia/commons/9/99/Attila_Museum.JPG

Marcian immediately revoked the treaties with Atilla the Hun and stopped annual payments. In Italy, Valentinian III's sister Honoria sent a desperate message to Attila, begging him to rescue her from a forced marriage her brother was negotiating. Attila interpreted this as an offer of marriage and a potential way to grab the western empire. In 452, he invaded Italy to claim his bride but only ended up plundering the land. While Attila was in Italy, Marcian slipped into the Hungarian heartland, defeating the Huns in their territory. Meanwhile, the western empire, beleaguered by famine and the plague, bribed Atilla to leave Italy.

In 455, a Vandal fleet sailed to Italy and sacked Rome, first knocking down the city's aqueducts. When they reached the gates, Pope Leo I made them promise not to destroy Rome or murder its people. The Vandals agreed, and the gates opened. The Vandals kept their promise – they burned nothing, and they didn't kill masses of people, but they plundered the city's treasures for two weeks and took captives as slaves – including Princess Eudocia, whom the Vandal king married. The Vandals conquered Sicily and menaced sea traffic in the western Mediterranean.

Western Europe was now ruled by a series of puppet emperors controlled by the barbarian warlords who swarmed the western empire. In 475, the Roman general Orestes, who had served as Attila the Hun's secretary and envoy, proclaimed his son Romulus Augustus as emperor – the last emperor of the west. Several months later, the barbarian Odoacer of the Ostrogoths (eastern Goths) invaded Italy, killed Orestes, and forced the 16-year-old Romulus to abdicate.

With Romulus' abdication on September 4, 476, the collapse of the western Roman Empire was almost complete. The remnant of a few western European states continued under some form of Roman rule for a few more years. Odoacer proclaimed himself King of Italy – the client of the eastern Emperor Zeno in Constantinople. In 488, Theoderic the Goth invaded Italy; after fighting for five years, Odoacer agreed to rule jointly with Theoderic. At the banquet celebrating the union, the Goths murdered Odoacer's men, and Theoderic hewed Odoacer in half. Technically, Italy remained under the authority of the eastern empire, but Theoderic was a law unto himself, King of the Visigoth Kingdom – a superstate stretching from the Danube to the Atlantic.

No single cataclysmic event ended the western Roman Empire. It disintegrated slowly, unable to cope with internal conflict, imperial incompetence, and the incessant hordes of barbarians. The eastern empire would continue into the Middle Ages as the Byzantine Empire, with Constantinople still the capital city. The city of Rome, although no longer the capital of a political empire, continued as the center of Catholic Christianity.

Conclusion

Ancient Rome left an indelible imprint on today's world. Traces of this remarkable ancient civilization still impact our legal and political systems, language, literature, religion, infrastructure, architecture, art, and technology. The Roman legacy survived the empire's collapse and continued to shape civilizations throughout the centuries. Rome's enduring legacy laid the groundwork for many aspects of today's society.

Classical civilization – the Greco-Roman world – emerged from the geographical regions that the Greeks and Romans influenced through literature, culture, politics, and religion. Greek philosophy, religion, art, medicine, astronomy, higher mathematics, engineering, and architecture strongly influenced early Roman civilization. Evander – Aeneas's ally, had settled the region that would later become Rome – bringing Greek political, cultural, and religious traditions with him. Alexander the Great believed Hellenistic (Greek) culture was the god's gift to mankind; thus, he felt called to export it to the regions he conquered – much of which later became part of the Roman Empire. Rome assimilated the Greek knowledge and worldview, then disseminated it through the empire and through the pages of history.

Galen – the Greco-Roman philosopher, physician, and surgeon – guided Western medical theory and practice for over a millennium. Ptolemy – astronomist, geographer, and mathematician – produced the *Almagest:* the most in-depth and enlightening astronomical-mathematical treatise of the ancient world, recording 48 of the 88 constellations recognized by today's International Astronomical Union. Hero of Alexandria – a first-century Greek mathematician and engineer – formed the Heron geometric formula and established the study of pneumatics and mechanics. Also in Alexandria, Diophantus – the Father of Algebra – wrote the *Arithmetica:* a series of books covering algebraic equations, geometry, and approximations. He was the first Hellenist mathematician who identified fractions as numbers.

Besides science and mathematics, the Greco-Roman world profoundly shaped literature, philosophy, and theology, which were preserved and passed on by the Christian church after the Roman Empire crumbled. The medieval Christian universities focused on Greco-Roman classics, including Boethius' *Consolation of Philosophy* and his translations of Plato and Aristotle.

Marcus Aurelius was the last of the "Five Good Emperors" but also a Stoic philosopher and writer.
https://en.wikipedia.org/wiki/Marcus_Aurelius#/media/File:Young_Marcus_Aurelius_Musei_Capitolini_MC279.jpg

Saint Augustine drew from Cicero, Homer, Varro, Virgil, and especially Plato in the *City of God* – his philosophical treatise about moral decay causing Rome's fall and comparing the "City of God" with the "City of Man," symbolic of the perpetual struggle between faith and unbelief. The Renaissance's syncretism of Hellenism with Christianity revived interest in the Greek and Roman philosophical classics, such as the writings of Marcus Aurelius, Epictetus, and Seneca the Younger.

"Innocent until proven guilty!" This well-known concept, which sprang from ancient Roman law, underlines the Roman influence on the western criminal justice system. The Romans set the precedent for today's court proceedings in modern judiciary systems. Like today's court system, the accused would have a preliminary hearing to determine just cause for a case. If sufficient grounds merited going forward, a formal indictment or charge would inform what the charges were, and a trial by jury would hear from the witnesses and examine the evidence.

The Law of the Twelve Tables, dating to 450 BC, contained the written laws of Rome engraved on 12 bronze tablets – the beginning of a codified system – permitting all citizens to know what the laws were and be treated equally. Before that, citizens often only found out about laws when they broke them and were arrested. The *Twelve Tables* focused on civil law – usually disputes between individuals, such as contracts or property damage, but the state also had public law dealing with things like taxes or treason. The Roman codified law system is the common foundation of today's systematic and comprehensive written laws.

Who made the laws in ancient Rome? During the Republic era, lawmaking involved two bodies of legislation (like America's House of Representatives and Senate). The *comitia* or assembly of citizens first passed legislation, which then went to the Senate for approval. This model of lawmaking continues today in most democratic governments.

Rome overtly influenced the United States in the realm of politics and government. America's founding fathers intentionally imitated the model of government used in the Roman Republic, including features such as a senate, checks and balances, vetoes, separation of powers in three branches of government, term limits, impeachments, quorum requirements, filibusters, and regularly scheduled elections.

The Romans left their mark on the Western world through the Latin language, used as the *lingua franca* (common language) throughout the empire. The Latin language gave birth to the Romance languages, including French, Italian, Portuguese, Romanian, and Spanish. Roughly one-third of English words derive from Latin root words, and another one-third comes from the Romance languages descended from Latin, especially Anglo-Norman and French. Latin words or Latin-derived words comprise

90% of legal, medical, and scientific terminology in the western world.

Some examples of English words derived from Latin are *scholar* for scholar, *cattus* for cat, *familia* for family, *Senatus* for Senate, *sermones* for sermon, *lingua* for language, *musicorum* for music, *cultura* for culture, *consensu* for consent, and *orbis* for orbit.

If you look at old Roman engravings on monuments, you will recognize most letters – the Roman alphabet is the prototype for the English alphabet and most European languages (although the Romans wrote everything with capital letters). The Latin alphabet evolved from the Etruscan alphabet, which derived from the Cumaean Greek alphabet, which came from the Phoenician alphabet, which descended from Egyptian hieroglyphics.

English literature is indebted to Roman influence. Examples of English classics inspired by Roman history or Roman literary style include Chaucer's *The House of Fame,* Dante's *Inferno,* James Joyce's *Ulysses,* Milton's *Paradise Lost,* Robert Graves' *I Claudius,* and, of course, Shakespeare's *Julius Caesar* and *Antony and Cleopatra.* Chaucer, Dante, Milton, and Shakespeare were all influenced by Ovid's *Metamorphoses.*

Throughout the modernist T. S. Eliot's satirical and complicated poetry are allusions to Greco-Roman myths, including Sybil, Hercules, Cupid, and Chronis. C.S. Lewis' works reveal a mind intimately familiar with Roman mythology and literature: *Till We Have Faces* is a retelling of the Cupid and Psyche story from Lucius Apuleius Madaurensis' second-century *Metamorphosis.* Lewis's friend J.R.R. Tolkien believed the pagan myths of Rome retained a semblance of eternal truth. In Tolkien's *Lord of the Rings,* Gondor reflects the eastern Roman empire with a Numenorean history that parallels Aeneas.

The Old Testament was translated into the Greek Septuagint version in Alexandra, Egypt, in the second century BC, and this is the version Jesus read from in the synagogue in Nazareth (Luke

4:16-20). Greek and Latin were the official languages of the Roman Empire; the New Testament was written in Koine Greek – the Lingua Franca of the eastern Roman Empire. Most people in the eastern part of the empire – and some in the west – could have read (or have read to them) both the Old and New Testaments in Greek.

Latin was Rome's original language and continued to be used for administration, legal affairs, and in the military, gradually replacing Greek as the major common language in western Europe. Many people in the western empire could not read Greek or understand it; therefore, parts of the Old and New Testaments were translated into Latin – as early as the first century after Christ.

Jerome was an ascetic who spent the last years of his life in a cave outside of Bethlehem translating the Bible into Latin. He is often pictured with a skull – symbolizing the struggle of the spiritual nature over the earthly nature. By Matthias Stom - Oeuvre du Musée des Beaux-Arts de Nantes, Public Domain.
https://commons.wikimedia.org/w/index.php?curid=10285609

Jerome was a priest who knew Greek, Latin, and Hebrew; sensing the need for a good Latin translation of the entire Bible – especially for the western church, he moved to a monastery in Bethlehem in 382 to start translating. Using the earlier Latin translations, he first translated the New Testament Gospels – Matthew, Mark, Luke, and John – into Latin. He then translated the entire Old Testament into Latin by cross-referencing the original Hebrew texts with the Greek Septuagint translation and – since he was in Bethlehem – consulting with the Jewish scholars there on difficult texts. He finished translating the entire Old Testament and the Gospels into Latin – in what's known as the Vulgate – by 405. It was called the Vulgate (meaning *commonly used*) because he used everyday, easier-to-understand Latin rather than scholarly, classical Latin (which he knew well but wanted a version the ordinary people could understand).

Jerome's new Latin translation of the Bible had its critics – but now the western empire had a Bible in a language they could read and understand. This aided the spreading of Christianity throughout western Europe. The Vulgate was the Latin translation used by the Roman Catholic church for centuries – right up until 1979. The Latin Bible helped grow the church; in return, the church preserved the Latin language through the centuries with Jerome's translation.

"All roads lead to Rome" reflected the days of the Roman Republic and Empire when the *Viae Romanae* or Roman roads traveled like rays of the sun from Rome to points throughout the empire – providing efficient travel for the military, government officials, merchants, and ordinary people. Roman roads still exist today, two millennia later; some even have their original cobblestones. Others have formed the routes for modern-day roads and highways.

Roman roads were constructed with a three-level substructure of dirt, gravel, and bricks with the paving stones on top made from rock slabs. They were amazingly strong and resilient, resistant to harsh weather, and built with a slight lift in the center to allow efficient rain drainage.

Rome's sweeping network of over 250,000 miles of roads was an extraordinary achievement for its day. They connected the colonies to each other and to Rome, enabling travel with wheeled carts. The roads had signposts marking the miles and the distance to the next town. One great advantage of the road system was permitting the Roman legions to travel by foot about 20 miles a day to quickly respond to uprisings in the cities or invasions on their borders.

Roman roads engendered another great invention used today – the postal service! The roads permitted relatively fast travel of messages from city to city, and they even had express delivery using horses.

Echoes of ancient Rome still resound in different spheres of life, more than we realize. Our calendar, holidays, philosophy, and sense of justice are part of the treasure trove left by the Romans. The rise and fall of Rome inspire us but also provide cautionary lessons we must learn for our survival. Ancient Rome still matters. Studying its history is still important: it continues to define our worldview, our self-concept, our spirituality, and our political ideals.

Here's another book by Enthralling History that you might like

Free limited time bonus

Stop for a moment. We have a free bonus set up for you. The problem is this: we forget 90% of everything that we read after 7 days. Crazy fact, right? Here's the solution: we've created a printable, 1-page pdf summary for this book that you're reading now. All you have to do to get your free pdf summary is to go to the following website: **https://livetolearn.lpages.co/enthrallinghistory/**

Once you do, it will be intuitive. Enjoy, and thank you!

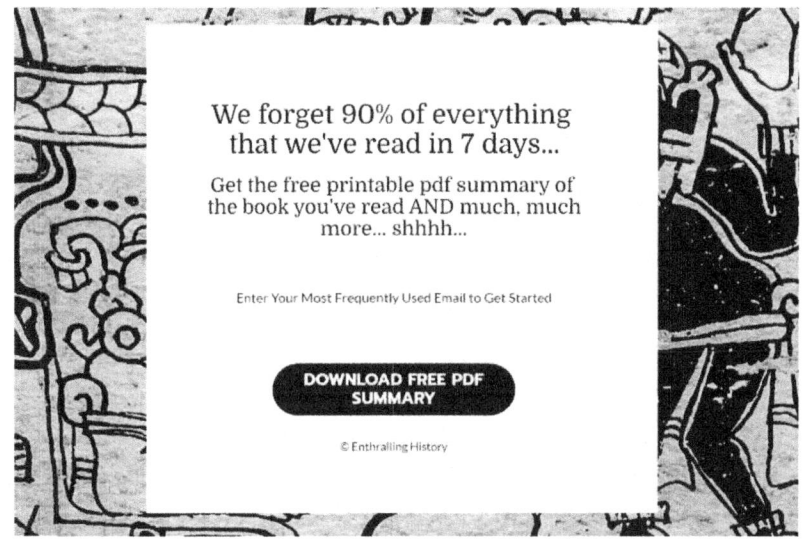

Made in the USA
Coppell, TX
05 June 2022

78505296R00136